Hit the
Ground
RUNNING

HIT THE GROUND RUNNING

A Spiritual Warfare Race

by

SHARON THOMPSON

XULON PRESS ELITE

Xulon Press Elite
2301 Lucien Way #415
Maitland, FL 32751
407.339.4217
www.xulonpress.com

All Scripture is in the New King James Version unless otherwise stated. Scripture quotations marked NKJV are taken from the New King James Version ©1985 by Thomas Nelson Inc. Used by permission. All rights reserved. Scriptures taken from THE AMPLIFIED BIBLE, Old Testament © 1965, 1987, by the Zondervan Corporation. The Amplified New Testament © 1958, 1987 by the Lockman Foundation. Used by permission. Scripture quotations marked KJV are taken from the King James Version. Scripture quotations marked Complete Jewish Bible are taken from the Complete Jewish Bible by David H. Stern. Jewish New Testament Publications, Inc., Clarksville, Maryland USA; © 1998 by David H. Stern. Scripture taken from the HOLY BIBLE, NEW INTERNATIONAL VERSION ©. Copyright © 1973, 1978, 1984 by International Bible Society. Used by permission of Zondervan Publishing House. All rights reserved

Images "Be Courageous" and "Firey Darts" ©Bill Osborne – www.BillOsborne.com. Used by permission from Bill Osborne.

Printed in the United States of America.

ISBN-13: 978-1-6312-9497-6

ENDORSEMENTS

In thirty years of ministry and as a denominational leader, there are those unique individuals whose passion and zeal for the Kingdom of God are above and beyond the ordinary. Sharon Thompson is a woman whose intensity to see lives changed and transformed by the power and word of God is evident in the fruit of her ministry. Sharon is straightforward, non-compromising, and practical in her discipleship methods. The Bible says that you will know a tree by the fruit it produces. Sharon has seen many lives transformed into fully devoted followers of Jesus Christ.

Sincerely,
Nick Gough, M.Div.
Senior Pastor
Faith Center, Great Falls, MT

As a pastor over curriculum I am always looking for something that I can put in the hands of new believers that is easy for them to understand, practical, and covers aspects of the Holy Spirit without scaring them away. This book does just that. The thirteen-week lesson plan is precise, giving you the basic concepts that are needed to start the race and run it with excellence. The thought-provoking questions at the end of each chapter solidify the teaching. Sharon's heart to transform new believers and make them hunger for more of the Spirit is a constant thread throughout. It is a must read for all believers, shoring up any gaps that may have been missed during their walk with the Lord.

Robin Gough
Administrative Pastor
Faith Center, Great Falls, MT

✠

Hit the Ground Running is a wonderful, practical, and very timely publication. Never before in history has the Church so needed to speak up and to speak clearly. This book does that and it tells you how to do it, with practical examples and inspiring heart-warming personal experiences. It's fuel for your fire, diligently gathered by the author, Sharon Thompson, so that you can let your light shine.

By the time you complete this book, you'll have caught the same zeal to use your ordinary gifts and abilities, while allowing and expecting God to come through in extraordinary ways. *Hit the Ground Running* will show how every Christian needs to live an unashamed, victorious life for Christ our King. This book explains how that everyone is a minister and the ministry looks like our lives.

However— CAUTION: Do not read this book if your desire is to be a spectator in the Kingdom of God. This book will challenge and change you... but equally important, it will leave you encouraged.

Denise Hartmann Echterling
Author, Speaker,
Evangelist with Hart to Hart Ministries

✠

As a pastor over many ministries and a business leader in the global marketplace, I highly recommend *Hit The Ground Running, A Spiritual Warfare Race*, as an essential resource for equipping and training new believers in Christ!

I have ministered with Sharon for many years. I am impressed at her ability to effectively communicate her heart's desire to develop and empower Christians through onsite training, one on one mentoring, and small group development!

This book is a timeless resource that will equip individuals, pastors and ministries to walk in the full power and authority God has given you!

Candra Oakes Niswanger
Pastor, Worship Leader, Songwriter,
Author, Motivational Speaker, Personal &
Business Coach
The Gathering, Great Falls, MT

✠

Sharon is a tremendous author. Her insight and wisdom come from a deep and abiding relationship with Jesus Christ. Sharon's knowledge of scripture has been gleaned from many hours spent in the word and study. You will be strengthened in your relationship to God through her writing. God bless you as you take this journey with her.

Pastor Jim Petty
Assistant Pastor
Hope City Church
Roanoke, VA

TABLE OF CONTENTS

ACKNOWLEDGEMENTS

I would like to thank my husband, Jim, for walking with me and the Lord for forty-nine years. For his encouragement to put this material into a book and for the hours he spent helping me on the computer.

I would also like to thank Pastor Robin Gough for her many hours of editing and wise council to bring this baby all the way through.

Also, I would like to thank Lori Bonifay for helping me with launching this into book format. I would like to extend a special thanks to Bill Osborne for allowing me to use his creative graphics for my cover page and armor of God.

INTRODUCTION

This book has been a long time in coming. It is the result of working with new believers for many years. I have seen a great need for giving people the foundational basic knowledge of the Word of God and how to practically apply it in their lives. These are biblically based truths that I personally apply to my own life every day.

We are to grow in the grace and knowledge of our Lord and Savior Jesus Christ (2 Pet. 3:18). I want to see you become strong in the Lord and in the power of His might...to be successful and victorious in every area of your life. May the truths in this book penetrate into your heart and lift you up into a new place in the Lord as you do what the Word says to do.

Be blessed, my precious friends.

Sharon

Chapter 1

WHAT IT MEANS TO BE BORN AGAIN

The New Birth

The New Birth is not: doing good deeds – doing your best – being cultured or refined – being moral — reading the Bible – saying prayers – going to church – water baptism – confirmation – church membership – the taking of sacraments – observing religious duties – or an intellectual reception of Christianity or any of the many other things some men are trusting in to save them.[1] When you received Jesus as your personal Savior and Lord, you were born again. That's what happened when you asked Jesus to come into your life.

The New Birth is a *new creation* from above – the direct operation of the Word of God and the Spirit of God upon your life – changing your spirit completely when you truly repent and turn to God. This *new creation* is brought about in this way:

- Recognize that you are a sinner, lost, without God, and without hope (Rom 3:23).
- Admit that Jesus Christ died on the cross to save you from sin by His own precious blood.
- Come to God, turning away from sin and confessing Jesus as your Lord – *and you shall be born again*. (The Holy Spirit will then make you a new creature – a new creation – cleansing you from all sin by the authority of the Word of God and by the blood of Christ which was shed to atone for your sin.)
- Believe from your heart and confess with your mouth that God does forgive you of your sins and that you are born again.[2]

Romans 10:9-10—that if you confess with your mouth the Lord Jesus and believe in your heart that God has raised Him from the dead, you will be saved. ¹⁰ For with the heart one believes unto righteousness, and with the mouth confession is made unto salvation.

It's not enough to just agree with this scripture, but to actually say the words out loud.

"Dear Heavenly Father, I come to You in the Name of Jesus. I ask You to forgive me of all my sins. Wash me and cleanse me. Thank You, Jesus, that You died for me. I believe in my heart, Jesus, that You are the Son of God. I believe that You were raised from the dead for my justification, and I confess You, Jesus, now as my Lord. I believe that You're coming back again for me. Fill me with the Holy Spirit. Give me a passion for the lost, a hunger for the things of God and a holy boldness to preach the gospel of Jesus Christ. I am saved; I'm born again, I'm forgiven and I'm on my

way to Heaven because I have Jesus
in my heart."

So...now you're probably thinking, wow,
what is that big word I just said...justification?
Justification means being pronounced righteous
and it also means you have been acquitted from
guilt. Isn't that great?

2 Corinthians 5:17 says, "Therefore, if
anyone *is* in Christ, *he is* a new creation; old
things have passed away; behold, all things
have become new." You now have a clean slate.
Born again means begotten from above.

> 1 Peter 1:23—having been born again,
> not of corruptible seed but incorrupt-
> ible, through the word of God which
> lives and abides forever.

You are a three-part being — the real you is
the spirit man on the inside of you. You live in a
physical body, and you have a soul, which con-
sists of your mind, will and emotions.

> 1 Thessalonians 5:23 AMP – And may
> the God of peace Himself sanctify you

through and through [separate you from profane things, make you pure and wholly consecrated to God]; and may your spirit and soul and body be preserved sound *and* complete [and found] blameless at the coming of our Lord Jesus Christ (the Messiah).

Okay, so now you're probably thinking, "Hmmm, what does that word sanctify mean?" Sanctification means the separation of the believer from evil things and ways. This is God's purpose in calling you to Himself and it must be learned from God as He teaches it by His Word. As you follow after the Lord by reading His Word and praying and being obedient to what He tells you to do, you will be developing godly character. The Holy Spirit will be helping you become the person God wants you to be.

Hebrews 4:12—For the word of God *is* living and powerful, and sharper than any two-edged sword, piercing even to the division of soul and spirit, and of joints and marrow, and is a discerner of the thoughts and intents of the heart.

The spirit man inside of you received eternal life from God.

John 3:14-16—And as Moses lifted up the serpent in the wilderness, even so must the Son of Man be lifted up, [15] that whoever believes in Him should not perish but[a] have eternal life. [16] For God so loved the world that He gave His only begotten Son, that whoever believes in Him should not perish but have everlasting life.

1 John 5:11-12 AMP—And this is that testimony (that evidence): God gave us eternal life, and this life is in His Son. [12] He who possesses the Son has that life; he who does not possess the Son of God does not have that life.

Colossians 1:13-14 AMP—[The Father] has delivered *and* [a]drawn us to Himself out of the control *and* the dominion of darkness and has transferred us into the kingdom of the Son of His love, [14] In Whom we have our redemption *through His blood,* [which means] the forgiveness of our sins.

God actually adopts us as His own children. Romans 8:15-16 says, "For you did not receive the spirit of bondage again to fear, but you received the Spirit of adoption by whom we cry out, 'Abba, Father.' [16] The Spirit Himself bears witness with our spirit that we are children of God."

In Roman culture, when you were adopted, you had more rights than a natural born son. Once you were adopted, you could not be sold, and you were guaranteed inheritance rights, whereas a natural born son could be sold by his father to someone else.

Ephesians 2:1-5–And you *He made alive,* who were dead in trespasses and sins, [2] in which you once walked according to the course of this world, according to the prince of the power of the air, the spirit who now works in the sons of disobedience, [3] among whom also we all once conducted ourselves in the lusts of our flesh, fulfilling the desires of the flesh and of the mind, and were by nature children of wrath, just as the others. [4] But God, who is rich in mercy, because of His great love with which He loved us, [5] even when we were dead in trespasses, made us alive together with Christ (by grace you have been saved).

1 Corinthians 6:19-20 states, "Or do you not know that your body is the temple of the Holy Spirit *who is* in you, whom you have from God, and you are not your own? [20] For you were bought at a price; therefore glorify God in your body and in your spirit, which are God's." So we want to live a life that is pleasing to our heavenly Father.

1 Peter 1:18-23 AMP—You must know (recognize) that you were redeemed (ransomed) from the useless (fruitless) way of living inherited by tradition from [your] forefathers, not with

corruptible things [such as] silver and gold.[19] But [you were purchased] with the precious blood of Christ (the Messiah), like that of a [sacrificial] lamb without blemish or spot.

[20] It is true that He was chosen *and* foreordained (destined and foreknown it) before the foundation of the world, but He was brought out to public view (made manifest) in these last days (at the end of the times) for the sake of you.[21] Through Him you believe in (adhere to, rely on) God, Who raised Him up from the dead and gave Him honor *and* glory, so that your faith and hope are [centered and rest] in God.[22] Since by your obedience to the Truth *through the* [*Holy*] *Spirit* you have purified your hearts for the sincere affection of the brethren, [see that you] love one another fervently from a *pure* heart.[23] You have been regenerated (born again), not from a mortal origin (seed, sperm), but from

one that is immortal by the *ever* living and lasting Word of God.

So you see, receiving Jesus as your Savior gives you eternal life – a home in heaven— translates you out of the kingdom of darkness into the kingdom of God, and we are to live a different kind of life than we did before. We need to begin to think the thoughts of God and begin living the way He wants us to. We do that by reading His Word and doing what it says. We can't live a godly life in our own power and strength—we need the strength of God's Holy Spirit to help us. We will be talking about being filled with the Holy Spirit in the next chapter. It is an absolute necessity to be able to live a victorious Christian life.

> 1 John 5:3-5 AMP—For the [true] love of God is this: that we do His commands [keep His ordinances and are mindful of His precepts and teaching]. And these orders of His are not irksome (burdensome, oppressive, or grievous).[4] For whatever is born of God is victorious over the world; and

this is the victory that conquers the world, even our faith.

[5] Who is it that is victorious over [that conquers] the world but he who believes that Jesus is the Son of God [who adheres to, trusts in, and relies on that fact]?

This faith is a living faith that comes out of your heart, not just out of your head. The Word tells us that we need to be doers of the Word, not just hearers (Jas 1:22). We need to be just like little children listening to their dad and doing what he says. Our Heavenly Father is a good daddy. He loves us and wants the best for us, so He will never ask us to do something that would hurt us or someone else. What He asks us to do is possible if we are filled with His wonderful Holy Spirit.

WHAT IT MEANS TO BE BORN AGAIN
IMPORTANT POINTS TO PONDER

1. Born again means: _____
   _____

2. 1 Thessalonians 5:23 is praying that the God of peace Himself sanctifies you completely; may your whole _____, _____ and _____ be preserved blameless at the coming of our Lord Jesus Christ.

3. What part of you receives eternal life from God? _____
   _____

4. What is the true love of God? _____
   _____

5. _____ _____ is the victory that conquers the world.

6. This word means being pronounced righteous and it also means you have been acquitted from guilt _____.

7. The separation of the believer from evil things and ways is called _____
   _____.

Chapter 2

BAPTISM IN THE HOLY SPIRIT

Equipment for Service and a Victorious Christian Life

A fter Jesus rose from the dead, He commanded His disciples not to depart from Jerusalem, but to wait for the promise of the Holy Spirit. The reason they were to wait was so they would be powerful witnesses for the Lord (Acts 1:4-11).

We need this same power today. Acts 2:39 states, "For the promise is unto you and to your children, and to all that are afar off, even as many as the Lord our God shall call."

Jesus said in John 7:37-39 that out of our innermost being would flow rivers of living water – the Holy Spirit. When you get the Baptism in the Holy Spirit, you are filled up and overflowing with His presence. We need to ask for the Baptism in the Holy Spirit (Luke 11:11-13).

Just like you received Jesus as your Savior, you opened your mouth and asked Him to be your Lord (Rom 10:9-10). You need to do the same thing with the Baptism in the Holy Spirit. God won't give you a counterfeit. He's going to give you exactly what you're asking Him for – the Holy Spirit.

Acts 2:1-18; 29-39 talks about how the Holy Spirit was poured out on the day of Pentecost and how the same thing will happen to those who ask for the Baptism in the Holy Spirit.

When we don't know how to pray, the Holy Spirit helps us to pray. It will be a "perfect" prayer because we will be praying according to God's will (Rom 8:26-27).

When we pray in tongues, it will bypass our understanding (1 Cor 14:14-15). We edify or build ourselves up when we pray in tongues (1

Cor 14:4 AMP). Our battery gets charged when we pray in tongues.

> Jude 20–But you, beloved, building yourselves up on your most holy faith, praying in the Holy Spirit

> Jude 20 AMP–But you, beloved, build yourselves up [founded] on your most holy faith [make progress, rise like an edifice higher and higher], praying in the Holy Spirit;

Ephesians 5:18 says, "And do not be drunk with wine, in which is dissipation; but be filled with the Spirit."

Being drunk is the devil's duplicate for being filled with the Holy Spirit. God's presence comes down upon us in a special way when we pray in tongues. In His presence is fullness of joy, so you won't need the alcohol or drugs anymore.

> Psalm 16:11- You will show me the path of life; In Your presence *is*

fullness of joy; At Your right hand *are* pleasures forevermore.

God wants us to desire spiritual gifts (1 Cor. 12:1; 14:11). 1 Corinthians 14:1 says, "Pursue love, and desire spiritual *gifts,* but especially that you may prophesy."

Before praying for the Baptism in the Holy Spirit, ask yourself, "Have I had any occult activity in my life like: Tarot cards, Ouija board, séances, hypnotic regression, crystal ball gazing, dungeon and dragons, Wicca etc.?" If so, repent of those things and ask Jesus to forgive you, because that kind of involvement will hinder you from receiving the Baptism in the Holy Spirit (Deut. 18:9-14).

Expect to receive this gift when you pray. The Holy Spirit will begin to move on your vocal cords and put supernatural words on your lips. The Holy Spirit gives the utterance, but man does the speaking. Acts 2:4; 10:46 says, "For they heard them speaking with tongues and magnify God." 1 Corinthians 14:2 states, "For he who speaks in a tongue does not speak to men but to God, for no one understands *him;* however, in the spirit he speaks mysteries."

Throw away all fears from foolish teaching that says you might receive something false. Luke 11:11-13 states the Father will give you the Holy Spirit, not something else when you ask Him.

Pray out loud:

Father, I believe what You say in Your Word is true. Jesus Christ is the Lord of my life. I'm asking You, Father, in Jesus' name, to baptize me with Your Holy Spirit.

Open your mouth wide – breathe in and tell God, "I believe I am receiving the Holy Spirit right now by faith." Don't speak a single word in your natural language after that. Just relax, take a deep breath and fearlessly, boldly, lift your voice, and make those supernatural sounds that want to come out, working your tongue and lips as if you were speaking English. Expect the Holy Spirit to give you words and speak them out loud. Remember, you won't understand the words because they are bypassing your understanding. Go right on speaking, praising God with those supernatural words until a free, clear language comes and you have the inner assurance that you have received.

Praying in tongues opens the door to the rest of the gifts of the Holy Spirit. The more you pray in tongues, the more fluent you will become and you will also find your spiritual sensitivity to the promptings of the Holy Spirit increased.

✠

BAPTISM IN THE HOLY SPIRIT
IMPORTANT POINTS TO PONDER

1. Baptism in the Holy Spirit is _____
   _____

2. Why did Jesus command His disciples not to depart from Jerusalem? _____
   _____

3. How do you build yourself up on your most holy faith? _____
   _____

4. What can cause people not to receive the Holy Spirit _____
   _____

5. How can we pray a perfect prayer? _____
   _____

Chapter 3

OPERATING IN THE GIFTS OF THE HOLY SPIRIT

I would like to share with you what happened to me when I got born again and received the Baptism in the Holy Spirit. **Wow**! My life literally exploded with the power of God! I was raised in a denomination that was very liturgical. By that, I mean it was "stand up, say this prayer, kneel down, then sit down," and used the written format to participate in the service.

I didn't have a personal relationship with Jesus. I wanted to, but no one knew how to share that with me. So, by the time I was twenty-one years old, I was pretty desperate for a relationship with God. I was in my first year of marriage and things were very unpredictable because my husband had a drinking problem.

He would get violent when he was drinking, and life was becoming very scary. I had one little boy, Jason, who was about nine months old. I knew I needed answers and the church I was going to didn't have any for me.

I was watching Billy Graham on TV one evening, while my husband was drinking in the kitchen. I listened very intently to the message Billy was sharing and when it came time to make a decision to receive Jesus Christ into my heart, I stood up along with the thousands of people who were doing the same on the TV screen. I prayed a "life-changing" prayer out loud with Billy Graham even while my husband was yelling at me from the kitchen, "What are you doing, watching that old preacher for?" Well, I asked Jesus into my heart and my life began to radically change on the inside of me.

I knew there was "more," but I didn't know exactly what that was! About a year later, we moved from Billings, Montana, to a little town forty miles west of us called Columbus. Now I was pregnant again, with our second son, David. My husband, Jim, was spiraling downward into a dark place with his drinking. This was driving me to search passionately for answers.

During this time, I had found a small group of women who were studying the Bible once a week. They started giving me books on being filled with the Holy Spirit, yet not one of them had experienced the Baptism in the Holy Spirit! I read with great interest Pat Boone's book, *A New Song.* It gave his story of living in Hollywood and how his family was starting to fall apart. At the end of the book, there was a prayer to pray and ask for the Baptism in the Holy Spirit. If Pat Boone's life could be radically changed, I certainly knew I needed that same kind of change!

I distinctly remember, it was a beautiful sunshiny day. I was sitting on my couch facing the front window. Before I prayed the prayer, I said to God. "Okay, God! I am going to pray this prayer, but I don't want just a little bit of the Holy Spirit! I want all You've got!"

Bam! My living room filled up with sunshine! Out of my mouth came a language I had never learned! I started running around my house, speaking like someone from the Middle

East! **Amazing**! Something supernatural had definitely happened to me!

A few days later, God sent a lady to my front door who was running for office and when I let her in, she noticed some Spirit-filled books on my table.

She said "Oh, I have read those same books, too!"

I was absolutely ecstatic that someone else knew about this new discovery I had made. She gave me some contact information that led me to find a little church in Absarokee, Montana, where the pastor and his wife had recently received the Baptism in the Holy Spirit. They were meeting on Sunday afternoons.

Yay! By now our second son, David, was three months old and a very big baby at that! He was 9lb. 9 oz. when he was born. He was a breastfed baby and I felt like that was all I was doing. Feeding this hungry, chunky little guy! Anyway, I hopped into our little green station wagon and off David and I went to find this wonderful group of Spirit-filled people.

God had sent someone by the name of John Vorhes all the way from Tulsa, Oklahoma, up to Absarokee, Montana to help train these new

Spirit-filled believers in the ways of God and His wonderful Holy Spirit. He had divine connections with Billye Brim, Oral Roberts and Kenneth Copeland.

I began to study the Word of God like my life depended on it, and it did! I learned that when you receive the Baptism in the Holy Spirit, you get a nine-gift package of beautiful Holy Spirit-given gifts. 1 Corinthians 12:8-11 says they are: The word of wisdom, the word of knowledge, faith, gifts of healings, working of miracles, prophecy, discerning of spirits, different kinds of tongues, and the interpretation of tongues.

The first gift I received was tongues when I asked for the Baptism in the Holy Spirit. Tongues are so powerful! When you don't know how to pray, the Holy Spirit will pray perfect prayers through you as you pray in your prayer language. (Rom. 8:26-28, NKJV) This gift is for all believers as Mark 16:17,18 says. It is a sign of those who follow Jesus – "And these signs will follow those who believe: In My name they will cast out demons, they will speak with new tongues; 18 they will take up serpents and if they drink anything deadly, it will by no means hurt them; they will lay hands on the sick, and they will recover." Praying in the Spirit opens the door to the rest of the Holy Spirit's gifts.

I decided I needed to find out how God wanted to use me in the Body of Christ, so I began a three-day fast. Now, mind you, I had never fasted a day in my life before, but this was an absolute necessity! I told the Lord, "I'm not going to eat until You talk to me and tell me how You want to use me." By the third day, I felt I was going to die, but I was determined not to give up.

Finally, the Lord began to talk to me. His voice was on the inside of me, like I was hearing someone talking to me in my head, but it definitely was God. He said, "I am going to use you in Words of Knowledge, Prophecy, and Healing." Okay! Now I really dove into the Word of God to find out what these gifts were all about.

This is going to be a very condensed version of how to operate in the gifts of the Holy Spirit. The main thing to be aware of is that the Lord **wants** us to desire spiritual gifts and to have the love of God working together with them. 1 Corinthians 14:1 NKJV, "Pursue love, and desire spiritual gifts, but especially that you may prophesy." We just need to ask the Lord to use us in the gifts of the Holy Spirit.

Since the Lord told me the three gifts I would be operating in primarily, I will begin by explaining about how the Word of Knowledge operates.

The Word of Knowledge is how the Lord will give a person a supernatural knowing about someone or something. Usually this gift is paired up with the gifts of healing and can also include a prophetic word of encouragement. Quite often the gifts are either paired up or come in three of them working together.

There are seven ways the Lord can give you a nudge that He wants to use you to operate in the Word of Knowledge.

1. FEELING them – a sharp pain in some part of your body, or a throbbing sensation; maybe numbness or strong emotion like fear or panic. Just be careful that your feeling isn't caused by some condition in your own body.

2. SEEING them. You might get a mental picture such as a body part – maybe a heart, head, or problem in the stomach.

3. READING them. You might see a word over someone's head, or across their front or back; maybe even seeing a word on the wall or carpet. It will look somewhat like a newspaper headline or a banner.

4. An IMPRESSION. It's like getting a mental impression that someone has a particular condition, or the Holy Spirit has spoken a word to you.

5. SPEAKING them. While you are praying or standing by someone, words that you hadn't really thought about saying tumble out of your mouth relating to a physical condition or problem you didn't know the person had.

6. DREAMING them. You may have a vivid dream or vision that has to do with a health problem, or some kind of solution to a critical situation.

7. EXPERIENCING it. This is similar to dreaming it, but you may have a vivid vision while you are awake. It may be so strong, that you are not just an observer, but actually a part of the happening.

I usually get a Word of Knowledge in the worship part of a church service. Sometimes I get two or three and I write them down on a sticky note so I don't forget them. It is important to be submitted to the leadership and ask them if you can release these words out loud. When these words are released, people are healed in the meeting without anyone laying hands on them and praying for them. These gifts are also invaluable tools that the Lord uses to bring unbelievers into the Kingdom of God. So be open to having the Lord prompt you while you are in the grocery store, or just walking down the street. When you get these promptings, just follow the "love flow" of the Holy Spirit and ask the person the Holy Spirit is highlighting to you if you can give them a word of encouragement. I find that the promptings of the Holy Spirit are just gentle nudges and can easily be brushed away. Ask the Holy Spirit for boldness and move out in courage to be a blessing to someone else who really needs a touch from God.

The Gift of Prophecy is an inspired utterance by a believer prompted by the Holy Spirit. Prophecy is words chosen by the Holy Spirit, not by the person's own learning. It is usually a spontaneous statement, either long or short. It is a flash, an inspiration, an intuition from the Holy Spirit Himself. Prophecy is a horizontal experience. It's man to man. It should strengthen our inner man and lift us up spiritually.

Gifts of Healings is a ministry of God's love for us. Usually the first sign a person has that God is really present is when they are healed. If you'll approach a person who is beaten down, who doesn't think God cares and doesn't have any faith, and you say, "Well, you may not have any faith, but Jesus loves you, whether you know it or not," wonderful things will happen.

The Bible talks about gifts of healings, plural, because there is more than one kind of healing. Basically, there are four types of healing.

First, there is healing from sin. This is the healing of the things that take place in our spirit which we are personally responsible for because we have sinned knowingly. We need to encourage people to repent, meaning to tell God they are sorry and then determining not to repeat that behavior again, with God's help.

If we've hurt our neighbor, we need to tell our neighbor, too.

One of the main things that will block someone from being healed is unforgiveness. Bitterness, resentment, and hatred are indeed very serious sins. There is a distinct relationship between these attitudes and physical illness.

The second type of healing is inner healing. This is dealing with emotional or mental problems people have that would cause them to go to a psychiatrist. I have found that taking people through prayers forgiving what others have done to them releases a tremendous power from God to them and brings inner healing to them.

The third kind of healing is physical healing. It is often connected to an inner healing. That is why it is so important to follow the guidelines of James 5:14-16. I usually read these scriptures out loud to them, anoint them with oil, and emphasize the importance of forgiveness because it can block us from being healed. We want to remove any kind of barrier so the person will get a straight shot from the throne of God.

The fourth kind of healing comes as a result of being set free from demonic influence. It is called deliverance. This healing will include using the gift of discerning of spirits. I don't believe Christians can be possessed by evil spirits, but they certainly can be oppressed in their minds or bodies. Sometimes this is a result of generational curses that are in their background. Just like in the medical field on a client intake form, they will ask the question of whether your family has a history of heart problems or diabetes. So the medical field is aware of sicknesses that travel down the generational line, but they don't know how to set the person free from it. They can only treat symptoms. If the root cause is not dealt with, which is a spiritual one, the person will not get free.

Discerning of spirits is when the Holy Spirit lets you know if there is a demonic spirit at the root of a problem, like the spirit of fear or hatred or trauma. Jesus taught us how to operate in this gift in Mark 16:17 and 18. He said to "cast them out!" That means you speak to the evil spirit and command it to leave in Jesus' name and it has to go! Luke

10:19 NKJV, "Behold, I give you the authority to trample on serpents and scorpions, and over all the power of the enemy, and nothing shall by any means hurt you."

Discerning of spirits also gives you the ability to see into the spiritual realm and see angels. It will help you know supernaturally if someone is trustworthy or not. It is not the gift of suspicion, but if you pay attention to the Holy Spirit in you, this gift will help you avoid making many mistakes. Some people call it intuition.

The Gift of Faith is having the supernatural ability to believe God in the face of contradictory circumstances. Like the time Jim and I were out in the middle of nowhere in eastern Montana, hunting. The truck battery died and there was no one anywhere around to help us. We had our second son, David with us and he was only a few months old. Jim still wasn't a believer yet and he was extremely frustrated at the predicament we were in. He tried everything he could think of.

Then I said, "Let me try something." The hood of the truck was up and I laid my hands on the battery and commanded it to work in Jesus' name. Jim was still sitting in the cab of the truck while I was doing this.

I shouted out, "Try the engine!" Nothing happened. I stood in front of the truck and said, "I don't care, I believe anyway!"

He tried the key again, and **vrooom**! The truck started! He ran around excitedly saying, "What did you do? Do you have a screwdriver?"

"No," I said. "It was Jesus!" The Gift of Faith was operating that day! Hallelujah!

The Working of Miracles usually is paired up with the Gift of Faith. The gift of the Working of Miracles is perhaps the most sovereign of all the nine gifts.

Elijah is heard saying these words in 1 Kings 18:24a, "Then you call on the name of your gods, and I will call on the name of the Lord; and the God who answers by fire, He is God." God created the fire, but the *worker* of miracles was Elijah. The creator of the miracle was God. The working of the miracles came through the faith of the prophet Elijah. There is a difference in the *working* of miracles and the *creating* of miracles. God is the Creator of the miracle, while He has to have instruments, such as you and me, through whom to work these miracles.

We can look for miracles to happen. Many Christians may never have been taught that God performs miracles in the **now**, but He surely does!

The gift of the Word of Wisdom is not a gift of wisdom, but a word of wisdom. It is not only a revelation from God, but it is something you say. You deliver it to someone. It isn't a Word of Wisdom until you speak it. You have to "say it."

This gift usually works with the Word of Knowledge. It gives you understanding of how to apply the Word of Knowledge that the Holy Spirit has given to you.

The Gift of Tongues is directed to God. It is your spirit joining with the Holy Spirit. You open your mouth and a new language comes forth. It expresses the inexpressible. It builds you up and touches your whole being. Jude 20 AMP, "But you, beloved, build yourselves up [founded] on your most holy faith [make progress, rise like an edifice higher and higher], praying in the Holy Spirit." How do you recharge a truck battery if it's dead? You plug it into a charger! That's what happens when you pray in tongues! You become super-charged with Holy Spirit power!

The gift of Interpretation of Tongues works in conjunction with the Gift of Tongues spoken in a meeting. First a person prompted by the Holy Spirit will speak out a condensed heart-felt utterance of tongues in a meeting. These tongues are different than the personal devotional tongue a person receives when they get the Baptism in the Holy Spirit. They are more intense and sound different than your personal prayer language.

Then there will be someone else who will give an interpretation of the tongues. Sometimes the person giving the utterance in tongues will also give the interpretation in English or the known language of the people in the meeting. It will not be a *translation*, but an interpretation, giving the sense of the matter. Tongues and Interpretation of Tongues together equal the same as the Gift of Prophecy. It is just another beautiful way the Holy Spirit expresses Himself through God's people.

When the Spirit manifests a gift of tongues through you, some of the words will start forming in your mind. Sometimes you can almost see the words or you feel the words and you start out by faith. It is an act of faith and you have to cooperate with the Holy Spirit.

I encourage you to be bold and ask the Lord to use you to bring glory and honor to the name of Jesus by being a yielded vessel and let the Holy Spirit use you to be a blessing to others. Acts 4:29,30 NKJV, "Now, Lord, look on their threats, and grant to Your servants that with all boldness they may speak Your word by stretching out Your hand to heal and that signs and wonders may be done through the name of Your holy Servant Jesus."

✠

OPERATING IN THE GIFTS OF THE HOLY SPIRIT
IMPORTANT POINTS TO PONDER

1. When you receive the Baptism in the Holy Spirit, you get a _____ _____ of _____ Holy Spirit-given gifts.

2. What are the nine gifts of the Holy Spirit in 1 Corinthians 12:8-11? _____

_____

_____

_____

_____

_____

_____

_____

_____

3. How do the gifts of the Holy Spirit begin to function in our lives? By _____

_____.

4. What are seven ways the Lord nudges us to operate in the Word of Knowledge? _____

_____

_____

_____

_____

_____

_____

5. There are _____ different kinds of healings. What are they? _____

_____

_____

_____

_____

Chapter 4

RENEWING THE MIND

How to Read the Bible

It is very important once you get born again and filled with the Holy Spirit, that you begin to read your Bible daily. It is God's word and you need to take it as if He is speaking directly to you. Make it personal.

> Romans 12:1-2 AMP–I appeal to you therefore, brethren, *and* beg of you in view of [all] the mercies of God, to make a decisive dedication of your bodies [presenting all your members and faculties] as a living sacrifice, holy (devoted, consecrated) and well pleasing to God, which is your

reasonable (rational, intelligent) service *and* spiritual worship.

[2] Do not be conformed to this world (this age), [fashioned after and adapted to its external, superficial customs], but be transformed (changed) by the [entire] renewal of your mind [by its new ideals and its new attitude], so that you may prove [for yourselves] what is the good and acceptable and perfect will of God, *even* the thing which is good and acceptable and perfect [in His sight for you].

Ephesians 4:22-24 AMP–Strip yourselves of your former nature [put off and discard your old unrenewed self] which characterized your previous manner of life and becomes corrupt through lusts *and* desires that spring from delusion; [23] And be constantly renewed in the spirit of your mind [having a fresh mental and spiritual attitude], [24] And put on the new nature (the regenerate self) created in God's image, [Godlike] in true righteousness and holiness.

We need to retrain our thought patterns to think the thoughts of God. We do that by spending time in the Word of God.

Psalm 119:9 AMP–How shall a young man cleanse his way? By taking heed *and* keeping watch [on himself] according to Your word [conforming his life to it].

Psalm 119:105–Your word is a lamp to my feet and a light to my path.

Joshua 1:8 AMP–This book of the law shall not depart out of your mouth, but you shall meditate on it day and night, that you may observe and do according to all that is written in it; for then you shall make your way prosperous, and then you shall deal wisely and have good success.

Romans 8:6- For to be carnally minded *is* death, but to be spiritually minded *is* life and peace.

Carnal means having the nature of flesh; i.e., sensual, controlled by animal appetites, governed by human nature instead of the Spirit of God.

I encourage you to look up these following great scriptures out of the Amplified Bible: Psalm 119:1-6; Psalm 1 focusing on verse 2; Colossians 3:1-10 and Colossians 3:12-16.

Set a regular Bible reading time. You should plan at least fifteen minutes daily. Have a notebook and pen with you and write down any passage that is meaningful to you. I always underline it in my Bible, too. If you can't underline in your Bible because you're afraid of marking it up, put it down and get one you can underline in.

Read your Bible expectantly. Expect God to speak to you out of it. I have these words written in the flyleaf of my Bible. **This is my Bible. This is God speaking directly to me** _____ (your name) _____.

Pray first before you begin to read. Ask the Father in Jesus' name to give you hearing ears, seeing eyes, and open the understanding of your heart so you can hear, see, and receive what He wants to give you out of the Word. In Matthew 13:13-16, Jesus was talking about people who had physical ears, but they were not hearing what He was telling them or understanding what He was saying. Their eyes were blinded to the truth as well—that's why I pray and ask the Lord for hearing ears, seeing eyes, and the opening of my heart to His Word. I strongly suggest you do the same thing.

> 2 Timothy 2:15 AMP—Study *and* be eager *and* do your utmost to present yourself to God approved (tested by trial), a workman who has no cause to be ashamed, correctly analyzing *and* accurately dividing [rightly handling and skillfully teaching] the Word of Truth.

How the Bible is Divided

The Old Testament contains thirty-nine books, and the New Testament contains twenty-seven books for a total of sixty-six books. The Old Testament has five different categories:

· **The Pentateuch** — the first five books of the Bible: Genesis, Exodus, Leviticus, Numbers, Deuteronomy

· **History** — The next twelve books include: Joshua, Judges, Ruth, 1 Samuel, 2 Samuel, 1 Kings, 2 Kings, 1 Chronicles, 2 Chronicles, Ezra, Nehemiah, Esther

· **Poetry** — Five books: Job, Psalms, Proverbs, Ecclesiastes, and Song of Solomon

· **Major Prophets** — Five books: Isaiah, Jeremiah, Lamentations, Ezekiel, Daniel

· **Minor Prophets** — Twelve books: Hosea, Joel, Amos, Obadiah, Jonah, Micah, Nahum, Habakkuk, Zephaniah, Haggai, Zechariah, Malachi

There are 400 silent years in between the Old and New Testament. The New Testament has four different categories:

- **History** — Five books: The four Gospels (Matthew, Mark, Luke, John) and the book of Acts
- **Pauline Epistles** — Fourteen books: Romans, 1 Corinthians, 2 Corinthians, Galatians, Ephesians, Philippians, Colossians, 1 Thessalonians, 2 Thessalonians, 1 Timothy, 2 Timothy, Titus, Philemon, Hebrews.
- **General Epistles** — Seven books: James, 1 Peter, 2 Peter, 1 John, 2 John, 3 John, Jude
- **Prophecy** — Revelation

I usually read some from the New and the Old Testament daily. If this is all new to you, don't try to read the Bible just like any other book. I suggest you begin with the book of John in the New Testament, because it is God's love letter to you. It will all speak to you.

Example Reading Schedule:

| Day 1 | John 1 | Ps 1 & 2 | Prov 1 | Gen 1 |
| Day 2 | John 2 | Ps 3 & 4 | Prov 2 | Gen 2 |

The best way I have found for getting the greatest blessing out of devotional reading is the practice of keeping a devotional journal. An ordinary spiral notebook will suffice; allowing a page per day, put the day of the week and the date on top with space for the text to be read. Include the books and chapters you plan to read from as the previous examples above. I circle the ones I finish reading that day. Another option is the many Bible reading plans you can find on the Internet. These can also be loaded on your smart phone for listening or reading anywhere. *Biblegateway.com* has many options for you.

The **S.O.A.P.** method is an easy way to get a lot out of your Bible reading time.

- **S** — <u>scripture</u> — Write out the verses that seem to speak to you to let the Word sink in.
- **O** — <u>observation</u> — What do you see in the verses? What stands out?
- **A** — <u>application</u> — What is God Saying to me? How can I apply the truth?
- **P** — <u>prayer</u> — Pray God's Word back to Him. Confess any revealed sin.

Journaling is your response to what you have just read by writing down the scriptures and your thoughts. It helps you ask the Lord what He is saying to you today. It is a wonderful way to begin to develop your relationship with the Lord and it also helps you remember scripture.

The Bible is filled with promises from God to His children. Are there any conditions to be met? Never claim a promise from God unless you intend to meet the conditions.

A Command to Keep

The Bible is filled with commands for God's people to obey. These commands are for our good: the keeping of them both lengthens and enriches our lives. As you come upon them in your reading, select the most important for your life at that moment and enter it in your journal.

A Timeless Example

The Bible is the greatest manual on human behavior ever written. It contains thousands of timeless principles for daily living that guide the believer and help him to know God's will.

Many Christians have failed to grow through inconsistency in their daily devotional lives. It is absolutely essential to get into the Word daily to keep fresh and filled with the Spirit. When we make this time a top priority, we will experience the rich blessings God has in store for us.

✠

RENEWING THE MIND
IMPORTANT POINTS TO PONDER

1. Romans 12:2 says ____ ____ ____ conformed to this world, but be _____ by the renewal of your mind.

2. How do we keep a watch on ourselves? ____
   _____
   _____.

3. _____ Word is a _____ to my feet and a _____ to my path.

4. We should read our Bibles _____
   _____

5. The best way for getting the greatest blessing out of devotional reading is the practice of

    _____.

6. The Bible is divided up into the _____

    _____ and the

    _____. It has a total

    of _____ books.

7. Your response to what you have just read by writing down the scriptures and your thoughts is called _____.

Chapter 5

WATER BAPTISM

W e believe in water baptism by immersion, because Jesus is our prime example. He submitted to John the Baptist in being baptized in the river Jordan and God the Father expressed His open approval of Jesus calling Him His beloved Son in whom He was well pleased. When He came up from the water, the heavens were opened to Him and the Spirit of God descended like a dove and alighted upon Him (Matt. 3:13-17).

The Greek word for baptism is *baptizo*, which means to dip or submerge. Sprinkling came into use because some leaders distorted the purpose of water baptism making it equal with salvation. Some believe every person has to be baptized to be saved. However, this is not biblically correct. It is not salvation through baptism, but salvation through confession of Jesus Christ as your Lord and Savior. Those on their deathbeds were taken to tubs, and those who could not be moved were subjected to pitchers of water being poured over them. Finally, the practice evolved to sprinkling. We believe in immersion, the same formula our Lord submitted Himself to.

Water baptism is not optional for the believer. Jesus clearly tells us we are to follow the Lord in obedience of baptism. Those who know Jesus as their personal Savior will want to be obedient to His Word. Jesus tells His disciples to take the gospel to the ends of the earth and to baptize believers (Matt. 28:19). Jesus says those who repent and follow the Lord in obedience of baptism are saved (Mark 16:16). The eunuch understood his need for water baptism, and Philip clearly told him the one condition under which he qualified to be baptized was a firm belief in Christ as the Son of God. Upon his confession of faith, Philip then baptized the new convert (Acts 8:37-38). The disciples of Jesus often baptized people who heard and believed in Jesus (John 4:1-2).

The Bible is filled with examples of believers who were baptized in water. Our Lord is the best example of our need to be baptized in water. He submitted Himself to the humiliation of this act and thereby testified of His subjection to the Father. The baptism of Jesus was a public one, which many people witnessed (Luke 3:21-22). New converts in the early Church were baptized in water. Three thousand who accepted Jesus were baptized in Acts 2:41. The Christians at Samaria were baptized in Acts 8:12. Paul was baptized upon his conversion in Acts 9:18. He later testified of that experience of water baptism before the Hebrew leaders in Acts 22:16. The house of Cornelius was baptized after that dramatic outpouring of God's Spirit upon them in Acts 10:48. Lydia was baptized, along with her whole household, after their confession of faith in Acts 16:15. The Philippian jailer, along with his whole family, was baptized after they accepted Jesus in Acts 16:33.

Various churches have different methods of water baptism. However, without doubt, the best means is to carefully follow the biblical patterns and examples. Jesus commanded us to make disciples of all nations, "baptizing them in the name of the Father, and of the Son, and of the Holy Spirit, teaching them to observe all things that I have commanded you; and lo, I am with you always, even to the end of the age" (Matt. 28:19-20).

Jesus was baptized by immersion (Matt. 3:16). There is but one baptism: "One Lord, one faith, one baptism" (Eph. 4:5). We must be careful to follow the commandments of our Lord concerning baptism.

The purpose of baptism is twofold. First, it is a sign that we have been saved. Peter says it is a figure or symbol of our salvation. However, he is careful to point out that baptism does not forgive our sins (1 Pet. 3:21). Only the blood of Jesus can save us as we confess our sins and ask Him to be our Savior (Rom. 10:9-10). Baptism is a testimony of our subjection and obedience to God.

Secondly, it is also symbolic of our death to the old way of life, our burial and our resurrection to a new life in Jesus (Rom. 6:3-4). In Colossians 2:12, Paul emphasizes this truth again. When we go down into the waters of baptism, we are identifying ourselves with Jesus in His death, saying we deserve to die because of our sins. We are also saying we are dying to our old way of life. Coming out of the water, we are saying we will walk with Him in newness of life. In baptism, we publicly present ourselves to Jesus for Him to live through us and for us to serve Him (Rom. 12:1). This is the reason why we do not baptize babies, because they are not at the age of accountability. Babies and young children are dedicated to the Lord, but not baptized.

For as many of you as were baptized into Christ have put on Christ (Gal. 3:27). Because we have been commanded to be baptized, we must obey. The Holy Spirit is given to those who obey (Acts 5:32). Obedience becomes the touchstone of our lives.

We will obey His commandments if we really love Jesus (John 14:23). His commandments are easy to obey (1 John 5:3). Our obedience is a testimony to unbelievers (1 Pet. 2:15; Matt. 5:16). Obedience is our entrance to heaven (Matt. 7:21). Obedience brings eternal rewards (Rom. 6:22). Jesus is our example in obedience (John 8:29; Phil. 2:8). We must be totally obedient to Christ (2 Cor. 10:5).

Jesus only left two ordinances for the Church. He first told us to observe the Lord's Supper, commonly known as Communion. In Matthew 26:26-30, Jesus demonstrated with the Passover meal that His body would be broken for us, providing healing for our bodies, and His blood would be shed as the ultimate sacrifice for our sins. The symbolism of the Old Covenant was about to be fully satisfied in Jesus' crucifixion.

> Isaiah 53:4-5 AMP- [4] Surely He has borne our griefs (sicknesses, weaknesses, and distresses) and carried our sorrows *and* pains [of punishment], yet we [ignorantly] considered Him stricken, smitten, and afflicted by God [as if with leprosy].
>
> [5] But He was wounded for our transgressions, He was bruised for our guilt *and* iniquities; the chastisement [needful to obtain] peace *and* well-being for us was upon Him, and with the stripes [that wounded] Him we are healed *and* made whole.

In 1 Corinthians 11:26 it says, "For as often as you eat this bread and drink this cup you proclaim the Lord's death till He comes."

The second ordinance is water baptism. Water baptism is a sacred rite with a specific purpose for the believer, declaring we have gone down into death symbolically with Jesus and been raised to a new life, leaving the old behind.

The word ordinance means a duty or charge to be kept from Strong's Concordance #4931. If we love Jesus, we will be obedient to His commands.

✠

WATER BAPTISM
IMPORTANT POINTS TO PONDER

1. We believe in water baptism by _____ _____.

2. The Greek word for baptism is *baptizo* which means to _____ or _____.

3. Was Jesus' baptism a public one? _____.

4. Is water baptism optional for the believer? _____.

5. In Matthew 28:19,20 Jesus commanded us to make _____ of all nations _____ them in the name of the Father, and of the Son and of the Holy Spirit, teaching them to observe all things that I have commanded you: and lo, I am with you always, even to the end of the age.

6. What is the purpose of baptism? _____

   _____

   _____

   _____

7. What are the two ordinances left by Jesus for the Church? _____

   _____

   _____

Chapter 6

PRAYING EFFECTIVELY

I f you want answers to your prayers, pray scrip-
turally according to John 16:23-24, which
says, "And in that day you will ask Me nothing.
Most assuredly, I say to you, whatever you ask
the Father in My name He will give you. [24] Until
now you have asked nothing in My name. Ask,
and you will receive, that your joy may be full."
Jesus told us to ask the Father in His name, so
let's pray the way He told us to pray. Whatever
you shall ask the Father in My name (Jesus) He
will give it to you. To get the ear of the Father,
just say "Father, in Jesus' name…"

One of the most powerful ways to pray
is to pray the Word. Find the scriptures that
cover your need and begin to pray them. God
watches over His Word to perform it. Jeremiah
1:12 AMP states, "Then said the Lord to me,

you have seen well, for I am alert and active, watching over My word to perform it."

Here are some scriptures for healing in your body:

> Isaiah 53:4-5 AMP–Surely He has borne our griefs (sicknesses, weaknesses, and distresses) and carried our sorrows *and* pains [of punishment], yet we [ignorantly] considered Him stricken, smitten, and afflicted by God [as if with leprosy]. [5] But He was wounded for our transgressions, He was bruised for our guilt *and* iniquities; the chastisement [needful to obtain] peace *and* well-being for us was upon Him, and with the stripes [that wounded] Him we are healed *and* made whole.

We pray:
– Thank You, Father, that Jesus took all my griefs, sicknesses, weaknesses and distresses upon Himself so I don't have to be sick. Thank You that with the stripes Jesus bore, I am healed and whole. I believe what Your Word says. I

believe I receive my healing right now because of what Jesus has done for me.

Psalm 103:1-5 and Matthew 8:16-17 are some other powerful scriptures to put in your mouth and speak them over yourself for healing.

Mark 11:22-24 KJV–[22] And Jesus answering saith unto them, Have faith in God.[23] For verily I say unto you, That whosoever shall say unto this mountain, Be thou removed, and be thou cast into the sea; and shall not doubt in his heart, but shall believe that those things which he saith shall come to pass; he shall have whatsoever he saith.[24] Therefore I say unto you, What things soever ye desire, when ye pray, believe that ye receive them, and ye shall have them.

John 15:7-8–If you abide in Me, and My words abide in you, you will ask what you desire, and it shall be done for you. [8] By this My Father is glorified, that you bear much fruit; so you will be My disciples.

1 John 5:14-15–Now this is the confidence that we have in Him, that if we ask anything according to His will, He hears us. [15] And if we know that He hears us, whatever we ask, we know that we have the petitions that we have asked of Him.

His Word is His will. That means you ask the Lord for things with the right motive of heart. God's will is revealed to you in His Word. His will is for salvation, healing, and prosperity and good things in your life.

3 John 2 AMP–Beloved, I pray that you may prosper in every way and [that your body] may keep well, even as [I know] your soul keeps well *and* prospers.

It is important that we believe we receive the things we ask for before we ever see any change – otherwise there will be no change. Hebrews

11:1 says, "Now faith is the substance of things hoped for, the evidence of things not seen."

Faith in Christ is defined in Colossians 1:4 AMP as, "[the leaning of your entire human personality on Him in absolute trust and confidence in His power, wisdom and goodness]."

You have to believe you receive the substance of what you are asking for before you ever see it with your physical eyes, or you will never see it with your physical eyes. See it with the eyes of your spirit man. Use your imagination. Let the Holy Spirit paint it on the canvas of your mind.

> Mark 11:24–Therefore I say to you, whatever things you ask when you pray, believe that you receive *them*, and you will have *them*.

Unforgiveness will stop our prayers. Make sure before you pray that you have examined your heart to see that it is free of bitterness or resentment—any unforgiveness towards anyone. Mark 11:25-26 talks about unforgiveness. If we have unforgiveness in our hearts, we will not be able to walk in the promise.

Three Steps to Forgiveness

Forgiveness is not based upon whether you feel like forgiving someone or not. We forgive because the Father forgave us first, and we need to forgive others or He will not forgive us.

> Mark 11:25-26–And whenever you stand praying, if you have anything against anyone, forgive him, that your Father in heaven may also forgive you your trespasses. [26] But if you do not forgive, neither will your Father in heaven forgive your trespasses.

> Ephesians 4:32–And be kind to one another, tenderhearted, forgiving one another, even as God in Christ forgave you.

1. Father, I forgive them as You forgave me.
2. I ask You, Holy Spirit, to cleanse my consciousness of the whole incident. 1 John 1:9 says, "If we confess our sins, He is faithful and just to forgive us *our* sins and to cleanse us from all unrighteousness."

3. I will treat them as if it never even happened. Isaiah 43:25 states, "I, *even* I, *am* He who blots out your transgressions for My own sake; And I will not remember your sins."

You can't do this in your own human strength, but the Holy Spirit will help you to walk in victory in this area. Trust is earned. Don't go back into an abusive situation. Have healthy boundaries.

Matthew 18:19–Again I say to you that if two of you agree on earth concerning anything that they ask, it will be done for them by My Father in heaven.

James 5:16 b AMP Bible–The earnest (heartfelt, continued) prayer of a righteous man makes tremendous power available [dynamic in its working].

We develop our relationships with other people by spending time with them, talking with them, and doing things together. That's what prayer is—developing your relationship with God the Father, Jesus, and the Holy Spirit—by communicating with them. Talking with God is prayer. He wants to fellowship with you. So, talk to Him!

✠

PRAYING EFFECTIVELY
<u>IMPORTANT POINTS TO PONDER</u>

1. How do we get the ear of the Father? _____
   _____

2. What is one of the most powerful ways to pray? _____

3. Whatever things you ask _____ pray, _____ that you _____ them, and you _____.

4. _____ faith is the _____ of things hoped for, _____ of things not seen.

5. _____ will stop our prayers.

Chapter 7

KNOWING GOD

~~~

We must truly know our God. Daniel 11:32b says, "but the people who know their God shall prove themselves strong and shall stand firm and do exploits [for God]." This *know* comes from the Hebrew word *yada* pronounced yaw-dah from #3045 in the ***Strong's Concordance***. It means to know by seeing, used in a variety of senses including observation, care, recognition and instruction, acknowledge, acquaintance, advise, answer, appoint, assuredly, be aware, etc.

Read Psalm 63:1-11 AMP

Matthew 6:33 AMP–But seek (aim at and strive after) first of all His kingdom and His righteousness (His way of doing and being right), and then all these things taken together will be given you besides.

Philippains 3:10-16 AMP- [10] [For my determined purpose is] that I may know Him [that I may progressively become more deeply and intimately acquainted with Him, perceiving and recognizing and understanding the wonders of His Person more strongly and more clearly], and that I may in that same way come to know the power outflowing from His resurrection [which it exerts over believers], and that I may so share His sufferings as to be continually transformed [in spirit into His likeness even] to His death, [in the hope][11] That if possible I may attain to the [spiritual and moral] resurrection [that lifts me] out from among the dead [even while in the body].[12] Not that I have now attained [this ideal], or have already been made perfect, but I press on to lay hold of (grasp) *and* make my own, that for which Christ Jesus (the

Messiah) has laid hold of me *and* made me His own.[13] I do not consider, brethren, that I have captured *and* made it my own [yet]; but one thing I do [it is my one aspiration]: forgetting what lies behind and straining forward to what lies ahead,[14] I press on toward the goal to win the [supreme and heavenly] prize to which God in Christ Jesus is calling us upward [15] So let those [of us] who are spiritually mature *and* full-grown have this mind *and* hold these convictions; and if in any respect you have a different attitude of mind, God will make that clear to you also.[16] Only let us hold true to what we have already attained *and* walk *and* order our lives by that.

Forget your preconceived ideas and come up higher in God. Moses knew God's ways, but the children of Israel knew God's acts. We need to know God intimately and know His ways. I heard someone recently say that intimacy means: *into me see*. I think that's a great way of expressing what the Lord wants to have with us:

a face-to-face encounter. Exodus 33:11a states, " So the Lord spoke to Moses face to face, as a man speaks to his friend." Other great verses to read are Psalm 103:7-18, especially from the AMP Bible. In Isaiah 55:8-11 we read that God's ways are made known to us in His Word, so we must hunger after His Word and expect Him to open it up and reveal Himself to us.

John 14:21,23–24 AMP–[21] The person who has My commands and keeps them is the one who [really] loves Me; and whoever [really] loves Me will be loved by My Father, and I [too] will love him and will show (reveal, manifest) Myself to him. [I will let Myself be clearly seen by him and make Myself real to him.]

[23] Jesus answered, If a person [really] loves Me, he will keep My word [obey My teaching]; and My Father will love him, and We will come to him and make Our home (abode, special dwelling place) with him.[24] Anyone who does not [really] love Me does

not observe *and* obey My teaching. And the teaching which you hear *and* heed is not Mine, but [comes] from the Father Who sent Me.

Paul's powerful prayers for the Ephesians are found in Ephesians 1:17-23. He encourages you to know the Lord by having the spiritual eyes of your heart opened. I pray these scriptures often and it has made a major difference in my understanding of the Word and coming to know the Lord more intimately. Ephesians 2:1, 4-7; 3:14-21 are also important to pray. It is vital to make a commitment to seek the face of the Lord every day.

Isaiah 40:28-31 AMP–[28] Have you not known? Have you not heard? The everlasting God, the Lord, the Creator of the ends of the earth, does not faint or grow weary; there is no searching of His understanding.[29] He gives power to the faint *and* weary, and to him who has no might He increases strength [causing it to multiply and making it to abound].[30] Even youths shall faint and be weary, and [selected] young men shall feebly stumble *and* fall exhausted;[31] But those who wait for the Lord [who expect, look for, and hope in Him] shall change *and* renew their strength *and* power; they shall lift their wings *and* mount up [close to God] as eagles [mount up to the sun]; they shall run and not be weary, they shall walk and not faint *or* become tired.

We need fresh manna from God every day to continue to be strong in the Lord. Matthew 4:4 claims, "Man shall not live by bread alone, but by every word that proceeds from the mouth of God." This means a continuing Word, not just the one we got yesterday. The Lord wants to speak a fresh word into your life every day; make time for Him. One of the great ways to get to know the Lord more intimately is to call upon His name.

Psalm 91:14-16 AMP–[14] Because he has set his love upon Me, therefore will I deliver him; I will set him on high, because he knows *and* understands My name [has a personal knowledge of My mercy, love, and kindness—trusts and relies on Me, knowing I will never forsake him, no, never].[15] He shall call upon Me, and I will answer him; I will be with him in trouble, I will deliver him and honor him. [16] With long life will I satisfy him and show him My salvation.

Proverbs 18:10 AMP–The name of the Lord is a strong tower; the [consistently] righteous man [upright and in right standing with God] runs into it and is safe, high [above evil] *and* strong.

There is no other name that is higher than the name of Jesus. In Hebrew, it is pronounced *Yeshua* and it means salvation. Below is a short list of some of the Hebrew names of God and their meanings. It is very powerful to speak the name of the Lord in Hebrew. There have been scientific studies done about the effects of speaking Hebrew words, and how they actually affect the molecular structure of things in a miraculous and powerfully positive way.

Expect the Lord to come and meet with you in a wonderful way as you call upon and meditate on His wonderful and beautiful names.

YESHUA: Salvation. Philippians 2:8-11, Complete Jewish Bible says, "He humbled himself still more by becoming obedient even to death —death on a stake as a criminal! [9] Therefore God raised him to the highest place and gave him the name above every name; [10] that in honor of the name given Yeshua, **every knee will bow** —in heaven, on earth and under the earth — [11] **and every tongue will acknowledge** that Yeshua the Messiah is *Adonai* —to the glory of God the Father.

ADONAI: Pronounced – A-do-ni Psalm 83:18 NIV, "Let them know that You, Whose Name is the LORD — that You alone are the Most High over all the earth."[3]

Mal-akh Pah-nav: The Angel of His Presence. Isaiah 6:9 NIV, "In all their distress He too was distressed, and the angel of His presence saved them."[4]

Eh-lo-heem Ts'va-ot: God of Hosts. Psalm 80:7 NKJV, "Restore us, O God of Hosts; cause Your face to shine, and we shall be saved."

Eh-lo-hay Ha-Sha-lom: God of Peace. Romans 16:20a NIV, "The God of peace will soon crush Satan under your feet."[5]

Ka-dosh: Holy. Isaiah 57:15 NIV, "For this is what the high and lofty One says – He Who lives forever, Whose name is Holy."[6]

El-yon: Most High. Psalm 9:1-2 NIV, "I will praise You, O LORD, with all my heart; I will tell of all Your wonders. I will be glad and rejoice in You. I will sing praise to Your name, O MOST HIGH."[7]

YAH: Psalm 68:4 NKJV, "Sing to God, sing praises to His name; Extol Him who rides on the clouds, by His name YAH, and rejoice before Him."[8]

A-do-ni Rof-eh-kha: The Lord Who Heals You. Exodus 15:26 NIV, "He said, If you listen carefully to the voice of the LORD your God and do what is right in His eyes, if you pay attention to His commands and keep all His decrees, I will not bring on you any of these diseases I brought on the Egyptians, for I am the LORD Who heals you."[9]

A comment on this scripture. This is in the permissive tense, meaning God did not actually cause all this to come on the Egyptians, but it came upon them because they chose not to be under His umbrella of protection.

✠

KNOWING GOD
IMPORTANT POINTS TO PONDER

1. To know means _____ used in a variety of senses.

2. What was Paul's determined purpose in Phil 3:10-16? _____.

3. Moses knew God's _____.

4. _____ are Paul's powerful prayers for the Ephesians_____ the Lord by having the _____eyes of their _____ opened.

5. We need _____ _____ from God every day to continue to be strong in the Lord.

6. How is Jesus name pronounced in Hebrew? _____ What does His name mean? _____

Chapter 8

SPIRITUAL WEAPONS

W hether we like it or not, when we get born again, we are enlisted in the Lord's army. Immediately we are thrust into conflict. Colossians 1:13-14 AMP says, "[13] [The Father] has delivered *and* drawn us to Himself out of the control *and* the dominion of darkness and has transferred us into the kingdom of the Son of His love, [14] In Whom we have our redemption *through His blood*, [which means] the forgiveness of our sins."

Matthew 11:12 states, "And from the days of John the Baptist until now the kingdom of heaven suffers violence, and the violent take it by force." Greek – *biazo* – means to use force. It expresses the earnestness that men must have in getting rid of sin, all satanic powers, the influence of the world upon their lives, and standing true when relatives oppose them. The fight we fight is a fight of faith. God has given us supernatural weapons to win it!

> 1 Timothy 1:18-19 AMP–[18] ...wage the good warfare, [19] Holding fast to faith (that leaning of the entire human personality on God in absolute trust and confidence) and having a good (clear) conscience. By rejecting *and* thrusting from them [their conscience], some individuals have made shipwreck of their faith.

> 1 Timothy 6:11-12 AMP–[11] But as for you, O man of God, flee from all these things; aim at *and* pursue righteousness (right standing with God and true goodness), godliness (which is the loving fear of God and being Christlike), faith, love, steadfastness (patience), and gentleness of heart. [12] Fight the good fight of the faith; lay hold of the eternal life to which you were summoned and [for which] you

confessed the good confession [of faith] before many witnesses.

Of course, there will be opposition to our stand for the Lord and it usually comes from the people we least expect (Matt 10:34-39). We need to remember our battle is not with flesh and blood but with principalities, powers, rulers of the darkness of this world, and against spiritual wickedness in high places. Remember, people are not your problem – it's the demon behind them that is your enemy. The Lord has given us power and authority over all the power of the enemy, so we should never be afraid of the enemy.

Luke 10:19–Behold, I give you the authority to trample on serpents and scorpions, and over all the power of the enemy, and nothing shall by any means hurt you.

Matthew 18:18- 19–Assuredly, I say to you, whatever you bind on earth will be bound in heaven, and whatever you loose on earth will be loosed in heaven. [19] Again I say to you that if two of you agree on earth concerning anything that they ask, it will be done for them by My Father in heaven.

Jesus has been given the name which is above every other name and everything has to bow to His name. Therefore, we need to use His name fearlessly against the enemy and he has to flee (Phil 2:9-11). James 4:7 NKJV tells us, "Therefore submit to God. Resist the devil and he will flee from you."

2 Corinthians 10:3-5 AMP— [3] For though we walk (live) in the flesh, we are not carrying on our warfare according to the flesh *and* using mere human weapons.

[4] For the weapons of our warfare are not physical [weapons of flesh and blood], but they are mighty before God for the overthrow *and* destruction of strongholds,

[5] [Inasmuch as we] refute arguments *and* theories *and* reasonings and every proud *and* lofty thing that sets itself up against the [true] knowledge of God; and we lead every thought *and* purpose away captive into the obedience of Christ (the Messiah, the Anointed One).

The Bible tells us to put on the armor of light (Rom 13:11-14). It also tells us to be strong in Him and in the power of His might (Eph 6:10-18). The three areas we have to do battle in are the world, the flesh, and the devil. 1 Corinthians 10:13 refers to temptation, James 4:7 references the devil, 1 John 2:15 and 17 comments about the world.

1 John 2:15-17 AMP–[15] Do not love *or* cherish the world or the things that are in the world. If anyone loves the world, love for the Father is not in him. [16] For all that is in the world—the lust of the flesh [craving for sensual gratification] and the lust of the eyes [greedy longings of the mind] and the

pride of life [assurance in one's own resources or in the stability of earthly things]—these do not come from the Father but are from the world [itself]. [17] And the world passes away *and* disappears, and with it the forbidden cravings (the passionate desires, the lust) of it; but he who does the will of God and carries out His purposes in his life abides (remains) forever.

Revelation 12:11–And they overcame him by the blood of the Lamb and by the word of their testimony, and they did not love their lives to the death.

1 John 3:8b AMP–The reason the Son of God was made manifest (visible) was to undo (destroy, loosen, and dissolve) the works the devil [has done].

Luke 4:18-19–The Spirit of the Lord *is* upon Me, Because He has anointed Me To preach the gospel to *the* poor; He has sent Me to heal the brokenhearted, To proclaim liberty to *the* captives And recovery of sight to *the* blind, *To* set at liberty those who are oppressed; [19] To proclaim the accept-able year of the Lord.

We are to use our spiritual weapons every day. When you get up in the morning, you put your clothes on. You wouldn't think of going outside without them! We need to be the same way spiritually. Put your armor on first thing in the morning. Wake up prepared – bushy eyed and ready! Romans 12:11 AMP tells us, "Never lag in zeal *and* in earnest endeavor; be aglow *and* burning with the Spirit, serving the Lord." Be like Jesus! Recognize your enemy.

John 10:10–The thief does not come except to steal, and to kill, and to destroy. I have come that they may have life, and that they may have *it* more abundantly.

Remember never to use your weapons against another Christian. Our battle is in the heavenlies (Eph 6:12). We have the power of the name of Jesus (Phil. 2:9-10). Binding and loosing is found in Matthew 18:18-19, and in John 16:23-24 we are asking the Father in the name of Jesus. Mark 11:23- 24 tells us to use your tongue to speak the mighty Word of God into your situations and let it cut asunder every entanglement.

> Hebrews 4:12–For the word of God *is* living and powerful, and sharper than any two-edged sword, piercing even to the division of soul and spirit, and of joints and marrow, and is a discerner of the thoughts and intents of the heart.

> Jeremiah 1:12 AMP–Then said the Lord to me, You have seen well, for I am alert *and* active, watching over My word to perform it.

> The Word is extremely powerful!

TAKE UP THE
SHIELD OF FAITH,
WITH WHICH
YOU WILL BE
ABLE TO QUENCH
ALL THE FIERY DARTS
OF THE EVIL ONE

Ephesians 6:10-18

Finally, my brethren, be strong in the Lord, and in the power of His might. Put on the whole armor of God that you may be able to stand against the wiles of the devil. For we wrestle not against flesh and blood, but against principalities, against powers, against the rulers of darkness of this world, against spiritual wickedness in high places. So ... we say... I bind you Satan in the name of Jesus Christ. I bind you principalities, and powers and the rulers of the darkness of this world. I bind and cast down spiritual wickedness in high places and render you harmless and ineffective in (insert you and your family's names), lives, and also over anyone else I would be talking to and sharing the gospel with today in Jesus name.

John 8:31-32

Wherefore, I take unto myself the whole armor of God that I may be able to withstand in the evil day, and having done all, to stand. I stand therefore, having my loins girt about with truth. Thank you Jesus, I put on the belt of truth, for I shall know the truth and the truth shall make me free.

I put on the breastplate of righteousness, for He who knew no sin was made to be sin for me that I might be made the righteousness of God in Him and I am what your word says I am (1 Cor. 5:21). My feet are shod with the preparation of the gospel of peace. Above all, I take the shield of faith wherewith I shall be able to quench all the fiery darts of the wicked. I put on the helmet of salvation and I take the sword of the Spirit, which is the Word of God, praying always with all prayer and supplication in the Spirit, and watching thereunto with all perseverance and supplication for all saints. Thank You, Lord, that You are my rearguard (Isa 52:12; 58:8).

✠

SPIRITUAL WEAPONS
IMPORTANT POINTS TO PONDER

1. The weapons of our warfare are not _____ weapons of flesh and blood but they are _____ before God for the _____ and _____ of strongholds.

2. Are _____ our problem? Who is our real enemy? _____ behind them.

3. We should _____ be afraid of the enemy! God has given us _____ over _____ the power of the enemy and _____ shall by any means hurt you.

4. Our weapons are _____,
   the _____ and the _____.

5. We fight the good fight of _____.

Chapter 9

AUTHORITY OF
THE BELIEVER

Jesus has given us power and authority over all the power of the enemy. Let's look at the following scripture in two different Bible versions. The comparison is interesting. Luke 10:19 KJV says, "Behold, I give unto you power to tread on serpents and scorpions, and over all the power of the enemy: and nothing shall by any means hurt you." Luke 10:19 AMP states, "Behold! I have given you authority *and* power to trample upon serpents and scorpions, and [physical and mental strength and ability] over all the power that the enemy [possesses]; and nothing shall in any way harm you."

Jesus spoke to demons and commanded them to leave and they left. He didn't *ask* the

Father to cast them out, He *told* them to go and they did.

> Mark 1:27–Then they were all amazed, so that they questioned among themselves, saying, "What is this? What new doctrine *is* this? For with authority He commands even the unclean spirits, and they obey Him."

> Mark 16:17-18–And these signs will follow those who believe: In My name they will cast out demons; they will speak with new tongues; [18] they will take up serpents; and if they drink anything deadly, it will by no means hurt them; they will lay hands on the sick, and they will recover."

These signs should follow all believers. Deliverance was a major part of Jesus' ministry; He has given us His delegated power and authority to exercise in the earth and establish His kingdom, His domain everywhere we go

Philippians 2:9-11 — Therefore God also has highly exalted Him and given Him the name which is above every name, [10] that at the name of Jesus every knee should bow, of those in heaven, and of those on earth, and of those under the earth, [11] and *that* every tongue should confess that Jesus Christ *is* Lord, to the glory of God the Father.

Matthew 28:18-20 — And Jesus came and spoke to them, saying, "All authority has been given to Me in heaven and on earth. [19] Go therefore and make disciples of all the nations, baptizing them in the name of the Father and of the Son and of the Holy Spirit, [20] teaching them to observe all things that I have commanded you; and lo, I am with you always, *even* to the end of the age." Amen.

Matthew 10:1 — And when He had called His twelve disciples to *Him,* He gave them power *over* unclean spirits, to cast them out, and to heal all kinds of sickness and all kinds of disease.

Matthew 10:7-8 — And as you go, preach, saying, 'The kingdom of heaven is at hand.' [8] Heal the sick, cleanse the lepers, raise the dead, cast out demons. Freely you have received, freely give.

1 John 4:4 — You are of God, little children, and have overcome them, because He who is in you is greater than he who is in the world.

2 Timothy 1:7 — For God has not given us a spirit of fear, but of power and of love and of a sound mind.

One reason why some Christians have so much trouble in their lives is they don't know the power and authority they have.

The first time we moved to Great Falls was in April of 1975. We lived out at Ryan Dam, which is about eleven miles outside of the city. When we first moved into the company housing, we were told that when it got really hot in the summer, the rattlesnakes would come down from the wheat fields into the cooler canyon where we were living. Well, we had two little boys at the time; Jason, who was three, and David, who was one year old. I had just read a testimony about a farmer in Canada who had walked around the perimeter of his land, declaring Luke 10:19 and proclaiming the power of the blood of Jesus. He took authority over rabid foxes so they would not invade his land. He soon found dead foxes on the borders of his land! I figured if it worked for him, it would work for me, since God is no respecter of persons. At this time I really learned about the authority of Jesus' name and the power in the blood of Jesus.

I walked around the perimeter of our yard, declaring that Jesus had given me authority to trample on serpents and scorpions and over all the power of the enemy and nothing would by any means hurt us. I also proclaimed the power of the blood of Jesus and said that no rattlesnakes could come into our yard. Confident that the Word of God and the blood of Jesus would protect us and my two little guys, I breathed a sigh of relief and went back into the house.

A day or so later, my little three-year-old, Jason came running into the house breathlessly stating that a snake was in the yard.

I said, "No, I don't think so. I've prayed, so that can't be!"

Little Jason said earnestly, "But, Mommy, there is a snake in the yard!"

I ran outside, talking to the Lord quite loudly, "Lord, I prayed!"

I distinctly heard the Lord say, "That is a bull snake, Sharon, not a rattlesnake."

I then vehemently began to shout, "I plead the blood of Jesus over our yard and no snakes, not bull snakes, water snakes, rattlesnakes, no kind of snakes can come into our yard!"

Whew! I learned I had to be specific when I prayed.

The next summer, we moved further up in the camp; that's what we called the housing facility where we lived. There were about twelve families living in company housing who worked for Montana Power at that time. Quite a few of the families had young children, so there was a lot of activity going on. I walked around the perimeter of our new place, declaring once again Luke 10:19 and the power of the blood of Jesus. We had planted a great strawberry patch in our backyard and it was covered with netting to keep the hungry birds away from the fruit.

Jason came running in one day, saying, "Mommy, there is a snake in the strawberry patch!"

I calmly said, "Now, we've been through this before. There can't be a snake in our yard!"

Jason just looked at me and said "but, Mommy, there is!"

So...I stormed out the door and grabbed the hoe, ready to slice and dice up this invader! I began to hack at the snake through the netting with angry, powerful strokes! *Ka-shwang, Ka-shwang*! There was no movement at all. I pulled back the netting with the hoe and there lay a snake that had been dead so long that rigor mortis had set in. I hooked him over my hoe and was carrying him triumphantly over to the cliff area where I was going to fling him as far as I could. My neighbor was just coming up from the garden area, wearing her cowboy boots as her protection from snakes that liked to curl up on the rock steps going down to the garden.

Her eyes got real big and she asked me what I was doing.

I gleefully shared, "See what happens to snakes that try to come past the blood line around our house! Jesus kills them!"

That was quite a testimony that spread like wildfire through the camp. My next door neighbor, who was extremely paranoid about snakes, had multiple snakes coming to her house, but they couldn't get into my yard alive.

Fear will draw the very thing you are fearful of to you. It is the opposite of faith. After she observed the power of the blood of Jesus and watching how we responded with love to hateful behavior directed our way, I was able to lead her to the Lord. The world needs a living demonstration of the power of the blood of Jesus and the authority He has given us to establish His kingdom in the earth.

Jesus told us to speak to the mountain in Mark 11:23-24, which says: "For assuredly, I say to you, whoever says to this mountain, 'Be removed and be cast into the sea,' and does not doubt in his heart, but believes that those things he says will be done, he will have whatever he says. 24 Therefore I say to you, whatever things you ask when you pray, believe that you receive *them,* and you will have *them.*"

We get what we say because God honors His Word—and His Word says that whoever says to this mountain (or problem), and shall believe that those things which he says will be done, he will have whatever he says. This promise can work as a two-edged sword: It can work for you, or it can work against you, depending on what you are saying.

> Proverbs 18:20-21 AMP — A man's [moral] self shall be filled with the fruit of his mouth; and with the consequence of his words he must be satisfied [whether good or evil]. [21] Death and life are in the power of the tongue, and they who indulge in it shall eat the fruit of it [for death or life].

You can actually weary the Lord by your words, as stated in Malachi 2:17a AMP, which says, "You have wearied the Lord with your words." Malachi 3:13 AMP proclaims, "Your words have been strong *and* hard against Me, says the Lord. Yet you say, What have we spoken against You?" When we have a negative pattern of speech and constantly use phrases like "I can't" and "I'm afraid," when God's Word tells us "I can" and "fear not," our words are out of harmony with God's Word and we are disagreeing with the Lord!

"Can two walk together, unless they are agreed?" asks Amos 3:3. We cannot walk with God in blessing, triumph, and abundant supply as long as we disagree with God's Word. Here is the secret: we have to agree with the Lord and say what He says about our life. We need to say what He says about our health, our finances, our strength, our anointing, our power; about all the blessings He has promised us in His Word.

It is true that if you believe what you are saying, then what you say is what you get! If you say, "I can't pay my bills," for instance, you won't be able to pay your bills—even though God's Word says "my God shall supply all your need according to His riches in glory by Christ Jesus," in Philippians 4:19. But, if you change your negative way of speaking and thinking, based on God's promise to supply, you will receive the financial miracle you need.

Since what you say is what you get, don't ever say anything you wouldn't want to get. Words are containers. They either carry life or death, just like Proverbs 18:20-21 says. So.... fill your mouth and words with life-giving power and reap an abundant harvest of blessing in your life!

Paul's message was with power and with the demonstration of the Spirit. We need the same demonstration and power of the Holy Spirit today.

> 1 Corinthians 2:4-5—And my speech and my preaching *were* not with persuasive words of human wisdom, but in demonstration of the Spirit and of power, [5] that your faith should not be in the wisdom of men but in the power of God.

The disciples prayed a very powerful prayer in the book of Acts that we need to be praying today.

> Acts 4:29-30 — Now, Lord, look on their threats, and grant to Your

servants that with all boldness they may speak Your word, [30] by stretching out Your hand to heal, and that signs and wonders may be done through the name of Your holy Servant Jesus.

Acts 4:33 — And with great power the apostles gave witness to the resurrection of the Lord Jesus. And great grace was upon them all.

The Lord tells us to desire spiritual gifts in 1 Corinthians 14:1. Therefore, it isn't wrong to pray and ask for spiritual gifts to increase in our lives. We truly should desire to be a living demonstration of the power of God moving through us to rescue a dying and lost world.

AUTHORITY OF THE BELIEVER
<u>IMPORTANT POINTS TO PONDER</u>

1. Jesus has given us power and authority over _____ the power of the enemy and _____ shall by any means hurt you.

2. Jesus _____ to demons and commanded them to leave and they left.

3. There are five signs that should follow believers. What are they? _____

_____

_____

_____

_____

4. 1 John 4:4 — "Ye are of God, little children and have overcome them; _____

_____.

5. The reason some Christians are having so much trouble in their lives is: _____

_____.

6. Proverbs 18:21 says that _____

_____ and _____

are in the power of the tongue.

Chapter 10

THE POWER OF THE BLOOD OF JESUS

O ne subject that is still a mystery to most Christians is the blood of Jesus. However, God *never* speaks of the blood as a mystery, so I believe He wants you and me to know all about the dynamite benefits that are ours through the blood. The answers to the question, "What *is* the power of the blood?" will revolutionize your Christian experience and produce powerful results on a day-to-day basis.

One of the strongest weapons against the devil we have is the blood of Jesus (Rev. 12:9-11). Specifically, Revelation 12:11 says, "And they overcame him by the blood of the Lamb, and by the word of their testimony; and they loved not their lives unto the death."

In Leviticus 17:11, God provided the condition for atonement by saying: "For the life of the flesh *is* in the blood, and I have given it to you upon the altar to make atonement for your souls; for it *is* the blood *that* makes atonement for the soul." It was the shed blood upon the altar, the death of a spotless animal that brought about the atonement or covering for sin. After it was shed, the animal's blood was sprinkled on the mercy seat – the golden lid on the Ark of the Covenant. The very presence of God was above the mercy seat by virtue of the shed blood sprinkled there.

Because the penalty for sin is death, the animal's death in the place of the sinner symbolized the ultimate sacrifice by Jesus for man's sin. According to Hebrews 10:4, the blood or death of bulls and goats was not sufficient to take away sins: an animal death was not an adequate substitute for the death of a sinful human – that required the death of a spotless human life – the life of Jesus.

The Bible says in Ephesians 1:7, "… we have redemption through His blood." To seal our redemption after His death, Jesus ascended to heaven, and through His own blood He entered the Holy Place once for all mankind and offered Himself to God (Heb. 9:12-14). Because of His death, we enjoy the benefits of God's grace and mercy, we enjoy His very presence, and we call ourselves Christians. It is faith in the shed blood of Jesus Christ that obtained God's favor for us, giving us a new name.

Jesus has redeemed us out of every tribe, tongue, people, and nation.

> Revelation 5:9b-10 — You are worthy to take the scroll, And to open its seals; For You were slain, And have redeemed us to God by Your blood Out of every tribe and tongue and people and nation, [10] And have made us kings and priests to our God; And we shall reign on the earth.

What does *redeemed* mean here? **Strong's Concordance** #59 defines "redeem" as – go to market; i.e., to *purchase*; specifically to *redeem* – buy.

> 1 Peter 1:18-19 AMP — You must know (recognize) that you were

redeemed (ransomed) from the useless (fruitless) way of living inherited by tradition from [your] forefathers, not with corruptible things [such as] silver and gold, [19] But [you were purchased] with the precious blood of Christ (the Messiah), like that of a [sacrificial] lamb without blemish or spot.

Galatians 3:13-14 — Christ has redeemed us from the curse of the law, having become a curse for us (for it is written, "Cursed *is* everyone who hangs on a tree"), [14] that the blessing of Abraham might come upon the Gentiles in Christ Jesus, that we might receive the promise of the Spirit through faith.

Galatians 3:29 — And if you *are* Christ's, then you are Abraham's seed, and heirs according to the promise.

Colossians 1:13-14 AMP — [The Father] has delivered *and* drawn us to Himself out of the control *and* the dominion of darkness and has transferred us into the kingdom of the Son of His love, [14] In Whom we have our redemption *through His blood*, [which means] the forgiveness of our sins.

These scriptures are so powerful! I try to take communion every day, and I speak Colossians 1:13-14 out my mouth several times, meditating on it before taking the bread and grape juice. I also use other scriptures about the power of the blood of Jesus at that time. They paint a wonderful picture of the difference the Lord makes between His people who have a covenant with Him, and the world who doesn't know Him.

The blood of Jesus has a voice and it speaks for us! Did you know blood has had a *voice* from the earliest of times in the Old Testament? It does! After Cain slew Abel, God declared to Cain. "What have you done? The voice of your brother's blood cries out to Me from the ground." (Gen. 4:10). The blood of Jesus has a voice. Hebrews 12:24 tells us it speaks "better things" than the blood of Abel. The "better things" declared by Christ's blood are words of mercy, whereas Abel's blood cried for vengeance.

No matter what your need may be, the blood of Jesus is speaking to God for mercy on your behalf. When you need reconciliation, the blood speaks for you; when you confess your sins, Jesus' blood speaks words of cleansing. Right now, the divine blood of Jesus is interceding with the Father on your behalf.

In Exodus 12:3-13 is the story of the Passover. The blood was applied to the two side posts and the upper door post. All in the house who took part in eating the lamb, bitter herbs, and stayed inside the house that was covered by the blood of the lamb were not touched by the death angel. If the firstborn had gone outside of the blood line, they would have been killed that night just like the firstborn of the Egyptians. **Jesus Is Our Passover Lamb**! He gave us a better covenant with better promises as indicated in Hebrews 9:11-28 AMP.

> Hebrews 8:6 — But now He has obtained a more excellent ministry, inasmuch as He is also Mediator of

a better covenant, which was estab-
lished on better promises.

2 Corinthians 1:20–For all the promises of God in Him *are* Yes, and in
Him Amen, to the glory of God
through us.

We need to be applying the blood of Jesus
to ourselves, our families, and all that we possess. We do that with the words of our mouth by
saying, "I plead the blood of Jesus over myself
and my family, home, job, etc." Pleading the
blood has nothing to do with begging. *Plead*
in the scriptures is legal terminology. It comes
from the Hebrew word *reev*. In the verb form
it means to dispute, controversy, case at law.
Examples of scriptures that use *pleads* are:

1 Samuel 24:15 — Therefore let the
Lord be judge, and judge between
you and me, and see and plead my
case, and deliver me out of your hand.

1 Samuel 25:39a — So when David
heard that Nabal was dead, he said,

"Blessed *be* the Lord, who has pleaded the cause of my reproach from the hand of Nabal, and has kept His servant from evil!"

It is interesting how these verses are worded "...has pleaded the cause...and has kept...from evil..." Just what we can do in pleading our case! Claim the blood of Jesus! Here are some other scriptures using this same terminology:

Psalm 35:1a — Plead *my cause,* O Lord, with those who strive with me...

Psalm 43:1 — Vindicate me, O God, and plead my cause against an ungodly nation; Oh, deliver me from the deceitful and unjust man!

Psalm 74:22 — Arise, O God, plead Your own cause; Remember how the foolish man reproaches You daily.

Psalm 119:154a — Plead my cause and redeem me...

Proverbs 23:11 — For their Redeemer *is* mighty; He will plead their cause against you.

Isaiah 1:17-18 — Learn to do good; Seek justice, Rebuke the oppressor; Defend the fatherless, Plead for the widow [18]"Come now, and let us reason together," Says the Lord, "Though your sins are like scarlet, They shall be as white as snow; Though they are red like crimson, They shall be as wool."

Isaiah 3:13 — The Lord stands up to plead, and stands to judge the people.

Lamentations 3:58 — O Lord, You have pleaded the case for my soul; You have redeemed my life.

The wonderful scripture below uses the Hebrew word *shawfat*, giving the meaning in this verse as: plead; have controversy together...

Isaiah 43:25-26 — I, *even* I, *am* He who blots out your transgressions for

My own sake; and I will not remember
your sins. [26] Put Me in remembrance;
Let us contend together; state your
case, that you may be acquitted.

Now we know what the Bible means by
plead. It is courtroom terminology laying claim
to our covenant rights purchased by the precious blood of Jesus Christ.

Some successful warriors I know take this
simple stand of faith: "I cover my home with
the blood of Jesus to protect occupants and possessions from any influence, Satan, that you or
your evil spirits would try to exert. I bring to bear
the power of the blood of Jesus to bind you." It
is also helpful to remind him God said what we
bind on earth He would bind in Heaven. The
applied blood of Jesus always calls his bluff.
He was stripped of his power at Calvary. He is
utterly helpless against the blood of Christ.

As God built a hedge around Job, which limited Satan, so today He will do the same for any
child of God who applies the blood to a given
situation. The blood is the hedge that stops
the destroyer. It is possible to be so hedged in
by this blood-protecting wall that nothing can

happen to you that is not God's absolute will. This is true in any area of your life. This principle can be applied to travel, to loved ones and to possessions. It is not a ritual. It is a living experience.

The scope of the sprinkling of the blood of the Lord Jesus is very great. It is not limited to people. It can be applied to things.

> Hebrews 9:19-21 AMP— [19] For when every command of the Law had been read out by Moses to all the people, he took the blood of slain calves and goats, together with water and scarlet wool and with a bunch of hyssop, and sprinkled both the Book (the roll of the Law and covenant) itself and all the people, [20] Saying these words: This is the blood that seals *and* ratifies the agreement (the testament, the covenant) which God commanded [me to deliver to] you. [21] And in the same way he sprinkled with the blood both the tabernacle and all the [sacred] vessels *and* appliances used in [divine] worship.

Exodus 12:7 AMP — They shall take of the blood and put it on the two side posts and on the lintel [above the door space] of the houses in which they shall eat [the Passover lamb].

Leviticus 8:24 AMP — And he brought Aaron's sons and Moses put some of the blood on the tips of their right ears, and the thumbs of their right hands, and the great toes of their right feet; and Moses dashed the blood upon the altar round about.

God told Moses to apply the blood in the consecration of the priests who were to minister to the people of God. "The ram of consecration...Moses took the blood of it, and put it upon the tip of Aaron's right ear, and upon the thumb of his right hand, and upon the great toe of his right foot" (Lev. 8:22-23). This was also done to Aaron's sons. The everlasting covenant dictates that all of us constantly need this covering. A blood-covered ear is needed to hear what the Spirit is saying to the churches. A blood-covered thumb is needed to render service to lost humanity and the Body of Christ. A blood-covered foot is needed to consistently walk in the Spirit.

I pray the blood of Jesus over my family, friends, pastors, and church every day. I always plead the blood of Jesus over my car before I leave the driveway and there have been very obvious deliverances from accidents. I encourage you to pray the prayer on the following page over yourself and your loved ones every day; begin to see the obvious protection of the Lord in your life.

-DAILY-
PLEADING THE BLOOD AND BINDING THE ENEMY

Father God, I plead the blood of Jesus over myself, my family, all my relatives and friends and their families, (name your church) members and their families, all the ministries and businesses we are partners with, and who are partners with us; over all the residents, employees, employers, students and those travelling in and out of (name your city) and its suburbs; over every major city and their suburbs in this nation, every town, and rural community; over every pastor and minister, apostle, prophet, evangelist and teacher in this nation, their families, churches, ministries, businesses, and possessions.

Satan, in the name of Jesus, I bind you and every principality, power, ruler of darkness, spiritual host of wickedness in heavenly places, every evil spirit, and every spirit that is not of God that has been and is now operating against us, I render you harmless and ineffective.

I cancel every hex, vex, spell, jinx, work of witchcraft, divination, black magic, psychic mind control, new age sorcery, and bewitchment sent to oppose us; I cancel every attack of oppression, depression, perversion, distraction, hindrance, and deception in Jesus' name.

I render every assignment, attack, scheme, and harassment of yours null, void, powerless, inactive, inoperative and ineffective against us in the name of our Lord Jesus Christ. No weapon that is formed against us shall prosper, every lying tongue is silenced, and every enemy that rises up against us is smitten before our faces and flees before us seven ways.

I cast you out of our lives, homes, circumstances, finances, and neighborhoods. Your works have been destroyed and we are free. Devil, everything you have stolen from us, I command you to repay us now sevenfold. I speak life to every area of our lives that you have tried to destroy: life, life, life, life, life, life, life in Jesus' name.

I cancel all hurt, harm, danger and accidents in our lives in the name of Jesus. I cancel all attacks against our families to bring strife, division, hatred, and rebellion, for God has given us peaceful habitations, safe dwellings and quiet resting places, and we dwell together in unity. I plead the blood of Jesus over us and all of our relationships; I declare we are growing in love and appreciation for each other in Jesus' name.

I cancel every attack of sickness, disease, pain, and infirmity sent against us, for Christ has redeemed us from the curse of the law and with His stripes we are healed. I cancel every attack against the finances of God's church, for we are the seed of Abraham and we are blessed above all nations of the earth. I call all the wealth of the wicked into the hands of the righteous, for money comes to us now! I declare this in Jesus' name.

I bind, rebuke, and cast out the spirits of fear, worry, doubt, anxiety, and unbelief, and give them no place in our lives. I pull down strongholds and cast down every vain and wicked imagination exalting itself against the knowledge of God and bring every thought captive to the obedience of Christ. I root up every plant in us that the heavenly Father has not planted and replace it with the image of God. I decree the Spirit of power, love, and a sound mind establishes our thoughts in the Word of God.

I loose into our lives the anointing of God to destroy every yoke and remove every burden; the Word of God in our minds, our mouths, and our hearts that God's kingdom will dominate the earth through us; we yield to the fruit of the Spirit and mortify the deeds of the flesh. I pray that the gifts of the Spirit will flow freely through our church to set the captives free and edify the church. I decree that God's people are enjoying the days of heaven on the earth now, in Jesus' name. Amen.

THE POWER OF THE BLOOD OF JESUS
IMPORTANT POINTS TO PONDER

1. What is one of the strongest weapons we have to use against the devil? _____ _____.

2. Jesus has _____ us to God by His _____ out of every tribe and tongue and nation.

3. What does redeem mean? _____ _____

4. The blood of Jesus has _____ and it speaks for us.

5. How do we apply the blood of Jesus? ____ _____

6. Pleading the blood is not begging. It is _____ terminology.

Chapter 11

WORSHIP

What does the word worship actually mean? According to the *New Strong's Complete Dictionary of Bible Words* – the word worship, or *shachah* in Hebrew, is used more than any other word for worship in the Bible – thirty-four times. It means to prostrate in homage. In fact, the first time we see the word worship or *shachah* is in Genesis 22:5, which says, "And Abraham said to his young men, 'Stay here with the donkey; the lad and I will go yonder and worship, and we will come back to you.'" Abraham and Isaac prostrated themselves before the Lord. Prostrate, from *Webster's Dictionary* means stretched out with face on the ground in adoration or submission.

The next most frequently used word for worship is *proskueneo*, which is used thirty-four times. It means to prostrate oneself. This is the word Jesus used in John when He was talking about worship.

> John 4:23-25 – "But the hour is coming, and now is, when the true worshipers will worship the Father in spirit and truth; for the Father is seeking such to worship Him. [24] God *is* Spirit, and those who worship Him must worship in spirit and truth." [25] The woman said to Him, "I know that Messiah is coming" (who is called Christ). "When He comes, He will tell us all things."

Proskueneo comes from two words – *pros,* which means towards and *kueno,* which means to kiss. Have you ever thought that when you are worshipping the Lord, you are kissing Him? When we are worshipping God, we are leaning toward Him to kiss Him! How wonderful! No wonder the devil wants to distract us from totally flat out loving God with our whole being!

Jesus was asked, "What is the greatest commandment?" He responded thus:

Matthew 22:36-40 — "Teacher, which *is* the great commandment in the law?"[37] Jesus said to him, "'You shall love the LORD your God with all your heart, with all your soul, and with all your mind.'[38] This is *the* first and great commandment. [39] And *the* second *is* like it: 'You shall love your neighbor as yourself.'[40] On these two commandments hang all the Law and the Prophets."

W. E. Vines Expository Dictionary of New Testament Words (Greek) gives the definition of heart: *kardia* – the chief organ of physical life. It occupies the most important place in the human system. In other words, the heart is used figuratively for the hidden springs of the personal life. Soul in the Greek is *psuche,* which denotes the breath of life. Mind in the Greek is *nous,* which means the ability of knowing, feeling, judging and determining.

This leaves nothing out, does it? Jesus says the Father is looking for people to worship Him who are totally caught up in Him...heart, soul, and mind, and our body is involved in this too.

There is a difference between praise and worship. Praise is celebration and very joyful. Worship is more quiet and reverential, experiencing the awe of the magnificent presence of the Lord Himself. It is not about the style of music, whether it is fast or slow, but about the attitude of the heart. Praise brings us from the outer court where we leave all our anxieties, worries, and concerns, and prepares us to enter the Holy of Holies where we enter into worship. You can praise God without music by speaking words of thanksgiving, proclaiming who He is. When you're in a worship service, you should move from praise into the Holy of Holies. Miracles can often occur during worship, as we give reverent honor to God. Many people have not experienced deep worship. Some are afraid to go there. The Lord longs for us to come and get lost in His presence – to worship Him.

When we love someone, it isn't just with our minds, with no outward expression, is it? No! We send cards filled with love words – we call them by special names of endearment – "honey," "precious," "baby," or "sweetheart." We hug on them, we kiss them. We love to look into their eyes! Let's get back to our first love and be "hot" for Jesus, our Father and wonderful Holy Spirit.

We sure don't want Jesus saying to us what He said in Revelation 3:15-16, "I know your works, that you are neither cold nor hot. I could wish you were cold or hot. [16] So then, because you are lukewarm, and neither cold nor hot, I will vomit you out of My mouth."

The following scripture is the blessing for the man, woman, or child who truly worships the Lord.

> Psalm 128:1-2 and 4 AMP — [1] Blessed (happy, fortunate, to be envied) is everyone who fears, reveres, *and* worships the Lord, who walks in His ways *and* lives according to His commandments. [2] For you shall eat [the fruit] of the labor of your hands; happy (blessed, fortunate, enviable) shall you be, and it shall be well with you. [4] Behold, thus shall the man be blessed who reverently *and* worshipfully fears the Lord.

Psalm 100 gives us instructions on how to come before the Lord. There is a protocol in every nation of how to come before their king or ruler. Jesus is King of all kings and our Father is the Creator of the universe along with Jesus and the Holy Spirit. It would be horribly insulting to the leader of a nation to come before him without knowing the proper protocol or manners for how to approach him correctly. How much more should we be acquainted with the ways of the Lord and how to approach Him!

> Psalm 100 — Make a joyful shout to the Lord, all you lands! [2] Serve the Lord with gladness; Come before His presence with singing. [3] Know that the Lord, He *is* God; *It is* He *who* has made us, and not we ourselves; *We are* His people and the sheep of His pasture. [4] Enter into His gates with thanksgiving, *and* into His courts with praise. Be thankful to Him, *and* bless His name. [5] For the Lord *is* good; His mercy *is* everlasting, and His truth *endures* to all generations.

Other scriptures about praise and worship include Psalm 47:1-9, which talks about clapping hands, shouting, sounding the trumpet, and singing. Also, Psalm 149 and Psalm 150 make references to singing, dance, tambourine, single or group dance, stringed and wind instruments or flutes, resounding cymbals – loud clashing cymbals. Let everything that has breath praise the Lord!

Holiness is returning to the church. The last move of God is bringing the church back to being a holy people — not legalism, but a holy reverence and fear of God…not wanting to do anything to displease Him because of our great love for the Most High God. The safest place to be in this hour is in His presence, abiding under the shadow of the Almighty, filling our mouths and hearts and minds with praise and worship. God inhabits the praises of His people. Psalm 22:3 KJV states, "But thou art holy, O thou that inhabitest the praises of Israel." It brings His tangible, manifest presence into our lives, and we are covered and protected by Him.

WORSHIP
IMPORTANT POINTS TO PONDER

1. What does the word worship actually mean?
   _____.

2. *Proskueno* means what? _____
   _____.

3. The greatest commandment is? _____
   _____
   _____
   _____.

4. What are some of the ways we get our body
   involved with worship? _____
   _____

5. In Psalm 100, how do we come before the
   presence of the Lord? _____
   _____
   _____

Chapter 12

REFLECTING THE CHARACTER OF CHRIST

Acts 11:26c — "And the disciples were called Christians first in Antioch."

C hristian — A word formed after the Roman style, signifying an adherent of Jesus, was first applied to such by the Gentiles as is found in Acts 11:26 and 1 Peter 4:16. The name means Christlike. 1 Peter 4:16 indicates the Holy Spirit considers it the highest name human beings can bear upon earth.

> 1 Peter 4:16 AMP — But if [one is ill-treated and suffers] as a Christian [which he is contemptuously called], let him not be ashamed, but give glory

to God that he is [deemed worthy to suffer] in this name.

The Bible tells us in Ephesians 5:1 to be an imitator of God. The word used here is the Greek word *mimetes* – which means to mimic the gait, speech, accent, and manner of life of another. We are to imitate God as children do their parents — imitate His acts, words, nature, ways, graces, and Spirit (1 Cor. 4:16; 11:1).

Ephesians 4:22-32 AMP–Strip yourselves of your former nature [put off and discard your old unrenewed self] which characterized your previous manner of life and becomes corrupt through lusts *and* desires that spring from delusion;[23] And be constantly renewed in the spirit of your mind [having a fresh mental and spiritual attitude],[24] And put on the new nature (the regenerate self) created in God's image, [Godlike] in true righteousness and holiness.[25] Therefore, rejecting all falsity *and* being done now with it, let everyone express the truth with his neighbor, for we are all parts of one body *and* members one of another.[26] When angry, do not sin; do not ever let your wrath (your exasperation, your fury or indignation) last until the sun goes down.[27] Leave no [such] room *or* foothold for the devil [give no opportunity to him].[28] Let the thief steal no more, but rather let him be industrious, making an honest living with his own hands, so that he may be able to give to those in need.[29] Let no foul *or* polluting language, *nor* evil word *nor* unwholesome *or* worthless talk [ever] come out of your mouth, but only such [speech] as is good *and* beneficial to the spiritual progress of others, as is fitting to the need *and* the occasion, that it may be a blessing *and* give grace (God's favor) to those who hear it.[30] And do not grieve the Holy Spirit of God [do not offend or vex or sadden Him], by Whom you were sealed (marked, branded as God's own, secured) for the day of redemption (of final deliverance

through Christ from evil and the con-
sequences of sin).[31] Let all bitterness
and indignation *and* wrath (passion,
rage, bad temper) and resentment
(anger, animosity) and quarreling
(brawling, clamor, contention) and
slander (evil-speaking, abusive or
blasphemous language) be banished
from you, with all malice (spite, ill
will, or baseness of any kind).[32] And
become useful *and* helpful *and* kind
to one another, tenderhearted (com-
passionate, understanding, lov-
ing-hearted), forgiving one another
[readily and freely], as God in Christ
forgave you.

When people look at us and our lives, we
want them to see Jesus shining out of us, and
that should be our aim in life—to be like Jesus.

James 1:21-25 AMP — [21] So get rid of
all uncleanness and the rampant out-
growth of wickedness, and in a humble
(gentle, modest) spirit receive *and*
welcome the Word which implanted

and rooted [in your hearts] contains the power to save your souls.[22] But be doers of the Word [obey the message], and not merely listeners to it, betraying yourselves [into deception by reasoning contrary to the Truth].[23] For if anyone only listens to the Word without obeying it *and* being a doer of it, he is like a man who looks carefully at his [own] natural face in a mirror;[24] For he thoughtfully observes himself, and then goes off and promptly forgets what he was like.[25] But he who looks carefully into the faultless law, the [law] of liberty, and is faithful to it *and* perseveres in looking into it, being not a heedless listener who forgets but an active doer [who obeys], he shall be blessed in his doing (his life of obedience).

Jesus' life was characterized by the fruit of the Holy Spirit.

Hebrews 4:14-15 — Seeing then that we have a great high priest, that is passed into the heavens, Jesus the Son of God, let us hold fast our profession. [15] For we have not an high priest which cannot be touched with the feeling of our infirmities; but was in all points tempted like as we are, yet without sin.

Galatians 5:16 AMP–But I say, walk *and* live [habitually] in the [Holy] Spirit [responsive to *and* controlled *and* guided by the Spirit]; then you will certainly not gratify the cravings *and* desires of the flesh (of human nature without God).

Also, read Galatians 5:13-15; 26.

We can apply our faith to have the Holy Spirit work in us and develop the fruit of the Holy Spirit by asking Him. Make a daily confession of Galatians 5:22. I pray, "Father, in the name of Jesus, I pray that the fruit of the Holy Spirit [that work which Your presence within me accomplishes] would be manifest in my life today in a greater way than it has been in the past...love, joy, peace patience, kindness, goodness, faithfulness, gentleness, and self-control."

Stay in the Word and you will reflect the character of Jesus (John 15:1-7).

Matthew 12:35 — A good man out of the good treasure of his heart brings forth good things, and an evil man out of the evil treasure brings forth evil things.

Out of the abundance of the heart the mouth speaks. Whatever you're putting in will come out.

Romans 8:6 — For to be carnally minded is death; but to be spiritually minded is life and peace.

REFLECTING THE CHARACTER OF CHRIST
IMPORTANT POINTS TO PONDER

1. What does the name Christian mean? _____
   _____.

2. Ephesians 5:1 tells us to be an _____
   _____ of God.

3. What does being an imitator of God look like? _____
   _____.

5. When people look at our lives, what should they see? _____
   _____.

6. We can apply our faith to have the Holy Spirit work in us and develop the fruit of the Spirit by _____
   _____.

Chapter 13

CHRISTIAN LINGO AND ABBREVIATIONS

You may hear the following words or phrases in church or around Christians. These definitions are simple. For more thorough definitions, refer to a Bible dictionary like *The Erdmans Bible Dictionary*.[10]

Agape – A Greek word meaning God's type of love that is unselfish.

Amen – So be it. Used to end a prayer or agree with someone's prayer.

Apostle–Sent one. Can be a leader of leaders, church planter, and or missionary. A leader in the church. (Eph. 4:11)

Atonement – Action done to cover sin by a priest in the Old Testament, ultimately leading to Jesus dying on the cross to remove sin. (Heb. 10)

Backbiting – Another word for gossip.

Bible Commentary – Explains the Bible verse by verse.

Bible Dictionary – Defines Bible terminology.

Blasted – See Slain in the Spirit.

Baptize – To immerse. Can refer to being water baptized or baptized in the Holy Spirit.

Born Again – When someone gives their life to Christ.

Brother – A male fellow follower of Christ.

Christ – Not the last name of Jesus. Actually means "Anointed One" or "Messiah" and refers to the one sent by God to save the world from being forever disconnected from God.

Christian – People who follow Christ.

Church – People who serve Jesus. Some refer to the building that the Church meets in as the church.

Demon – Evil spirit beings. Most likely angels that turned against God.

Disciples – Twelve men Jesus called to personally follow Him; Simon called Peter, Andrew, James, John, Phillip, Bartholomew, Matthew, Thomas, James the son of Alphaeus, Simon, Judas the son of James, and Judas Iscariot.

Evangelist – Leader in church that is focused on leading people to Christ, revival, or training people in leading people to Christ.

Gospel – (of the kingdom) "Good news" about God's kingdom coming here.

Gospels – The first four books in the New Testament; Matthew, Mark, Luke, and John.

Grounded in the Word – Deeply familiar with what the Bible says.

Hallelujah – Same as saying "praise God."

Harvest – New believers; reaping what is sown.

Heaven – Eternal habitation of God, angels, and followers of Christ.

Hell – Place designed for the devil and those that follow Him.

In Jesus' Name – Accessing the provision of Christ (John 16:23). Also, a typical ending in prayer. (In Jesus' name, Amen.)

Lost – A description of people before they become followers of Christ.

Messiah – Savior or liberator. Jesus is the Messiah of the world.

Pastor – Someone leading a local church. (Eph. 4:11)

Pharisee – Religious leaders in Jesus' day. Also, see Religious Spirit.

Plead the Blood – Claiming the provisions given through the death of Jesus.

Prophecy – Recorded messages from God.

Prophesy – The act of telling someone a message from God.

Quiet Time – Time set aside for prayer, reading the Bible and listening to God.

Prophet – Leader in the church (Eph. 4:11). Someone God calls to give God's insight to the Church at large. It is different from prophesying.

Rapture – Greek word for being "caught up" (1 Thess. 4:16).

Religious Spirit – An attitude of pride in religious or moral actions (Matt. 23:27-28).

Revival – Reviving what is dead. Could be special services at a church building where there is a supernatural increase of God's presence that leads to many people committing their lives to Christ and changes a community.

Sabbath – A day and a state of rest. (Ex. 20:8, Heb. 4:1-11) The Old Testament has this as a day, namely Saturday. When Jesus was raised from the dead on Sunday, much of the Church began calling Sunday the Sabbath (Matt. 28:1). Hebrews 4 speaks of the Sabbath rest as a position we have in God of being "at rest." In a relationship with God, you no longer have to strive for a sense of rest. You merely need to receive this sense of rest and no longer be anxious again. (Phil. 4:6)

Saint – Someone forgiven by Christ and following Him.

Sanctified – Set apart for God. Can do with holiness or being called by God to do something.

Saved – Someone who has become a follower of Christ.

Shepherd – Another word for pastor.

Sinner – Someone who has broken the laws of God.

Sister – A female fellow follower of Christ.

Slain in the Spirit – Where someone cannot stand up because the power of the Holy Spirit is on their body.

Strong's Concordance – Book that lists out many words and where they can be found in the Bible as well as the definitions in their original languages.

Teacher – Leader in the church. (Eph. 4:11) Someone who instructs people in the deep truths of the Bible.

Ten Commandments – Rules given by God.

Tithe – A tenth of our earnings given to God through the local church.

Trinity – One God in expressing Himself as Father, Son (Jesus), and Holy Spirit.

Washed in the Blood – Forgiven of sins.

Word – The Bible, prophecy, and Jesus.

Abbreviations for the books of the Bible
Old Testament (OT)

Abbreviation:	Book:
Gen	Genesis
Exod	Exodus
Lev	Leviticus
Num	Numbers
Deut	Deuteronomy
Josh	Joshua
Judg	Judges
Ruth	Ruth
1 Sam	1 Samuel
2 Sam	2 Samuel
1 Kings	1 Kings
2 Kings	2 Kings
1 Chron	1 Chronicles
2 Chron	2 Chronicles
Ezra	Ezra
Neh	Nehemiah
Esth	Esther
Job	Job
Ps	Psalms
Prov	Proverbs
Eccles	Ecclesiastes
Song of Sol	Song of Solomon
Isa	Isaiah
Jer	Jeremiah

Lam	Lamentations
Ezek	Ezekiel
Dan	Daniel
Hos	Hosea
Joel	Joel
Amos	Amos
Obad	Obadiah
Jon	Jonah
Mic	Micah
Nah	Nahum
Hab	Habakkuk
Zeph	Zephaniah
Hag	Haggai
Zech	Zechariah
Mal	Malachi

New Testament (NT) Abbreviations

Abbreviation:	**Book:**
Matt	Matthew
Mark	Mark
Luke	Luke
John	John
Acts	Acts
Rom	Romans
1 Cor	1 Corinthians
2 Cor	2 Corinthians
Gal	Galatians
Eph	Ephesians

Phil	Philippians
Col	Colossians
1 Thess	1 Thessalonians
2 Thess	2 Thessalonians
1 Tim	1 Timothy
2 Tim	2 Timothy
Tit	Titus
Philem	Philemon
Heb	Hebrews
Jas	James
1 Pet	1 Peter
2 Pet	2 Peter
1 John	1 John
2 John	2 John
3 John	3 John
Jude	Jude
Rev	Revelation

ANSWER KEY

Chapter 1

1. Begotten from above or a new creation
2. Spirit, soul and body
3. Spirit man inside of you.
4. That we do His commands 1 John 5:3-5
5. Our faith
6. Justification

7. Sanctification

Chapter 2

1. Equipment for service and a victorious Christian life
2. To wait for the promise of the Holy Spirit
3. Praying in the Holy Spirit.
4. Being involved in occult activity
5. Praying in the Holy Spirit. Romans 8:26 -27

Chapter 3

1. Gift package, nine.
2. Word of Wisdom, Word of Knowledge, Faith, Gifts of Healings, Working of Miracles, Prophecy, Discerning of Spirits, Different Kinds of Tongues, Interpretation of Tongues.
3. By asking the Lord to use us.
4. Feeling them. Seeing them. Reading them. Impression. Speaking them. Dreaming them. Experiencing them.
5. Four. Healing of Sin. Inner Healing. Physical Healing. Deliverance.

Chapter 4

1. Do not be – transformed
2. Conforming our lives to the Word of God

3. Your, lamp, light
4. Expectantly and daily
5. A devotional journal
6. Old Testament, New Testament, 66 books
7. Journaling.

Chapter 5

1. Immersion
2. Dip or submerge
3. Yes
4. No
5. Disciples, baptizing.
6. a. It is a sign that we have been saved.
   b. Symbolic of our death to the old way of life, our burial and our resurrection to a new life in Jesus.
7. a. The Lord's Supper — Communion
   b. Water Baptism

Chapter 6

1. Father, in Jesus' name
2. Pray the Word.
3. When you, believe, receive, will have them
4. Now, substance, evidence
5. Unforgiveness

Chapter 7

1. By seeing
2. That I may know Him
3. Ways
4. Ephesians 1:17-23, to come to know, spiritual, heart
5. Fresh manna
6. Yeshua, salvation

Chapter 8

1. Physical, mighty, overthrow, destruction
2. People, demons
3. Never, authority (power) all, nothing
4. Word of God, blood of Jesus, Name of Jesus
5. Faith

Chapter 9

1. All, nothing
2. Spoke
3. a. cast out demons
   b. speak with new tongues
   c. take up serpents
   d. drink any deadly thing, it shall not hurt them
   e. lay hands on the sick, and they shall recover
4. Because greater is He that is in you, than he that is in the world

5. They don't know the power and authority they have
6. Death, life

Chapter 10
1. The blood of Jesus.
2. Redeemed, blood
3. Purchase, buy
4. A voice
5. Words of our mouth
6. Legal

Chapter 11
1. To prostrate in homage
2. To kiss
3. Loving the Lord your God with all you heart, all your soul, and all your mind
4. Clapping hands, shouting, singing, dance, tambourine, trumpet, wind instruments, cymbals
5. With singing

Chapter 12
1. Christlike
2. Imitator
3. We imitate God's ways, acts, words, graces and spirit

4. Jesus shining out of us.
5. By asking Him to do that

CONTACT
INFORMATION

For more information about Sharon's ministry and involvement opportunities, contact Sharon Thompson at:

st.hitthegroundrunning@outlook.com

Find us on Facebook at Hit The Ground Running

ENDNOTES

1   Kenneth Hagin, *The New Birth*, Rhema Bible Church (Tulsa, OK: Hagin Ministries), 3.

2   Hagin, 17

3   Barri Cae Mallin & Shmuel Wolkenfeld, *Intimate Moments with the Hebrew names of God* (Gainsville, FL: Bridge-Logos Publishers, 2001), 10.

4   Mallin, 42.

5   Mallin, 56.

6   Mallin, 66.

7   Mallin, 148.

8   Mallin, 192.

9   Mallin, 134.

10   Benjamin & Micah Joy Williams, *The Basics in 21 Days*, Tate Publishing & Ent., LLC (Mustang, OK), 150-155.

CPSIA information can be obtained
at www.ICGtesting.com
Printed in the USA
BVHW091152040221
599034BV00006B/31